Fighting the Good Fight?

Socialist History 7

Edited by Willie Thompson, David Parker,
Mike Waite and David Morgan

LONDON • EAST HAVEN, CT

Published 1995 by Pluto Press
345 Archway Road
London N6 5AA
and 140 Commerce Street
East Haven, CT 06512, USA

Copyright © Socialist History Society 1995

The right of the contributors to be identified as the authors of this work has been asserted by them in accordance with the Copyright, Designs and Patents Act 1988

British Library Cataloguing in Publication Data
A catalogue record for this book is available from the British Library

ISBN 0 7453 1061 3

Designed and produced for Pluto Press by
Chase Production Services, Chipping Norton, OX7 5QR
Typeset from disk by Stanford DTP Services, Milton Keynes
Printed in the EC by Watkiss Studios

*The Journal of the
Socialist History Society*

ISSN 0969–4331

1. A BOURGEOIS REVOLUTION
Seventeeth-century England
1993, ISBN 0 7453 0805 8

2. WHAT WAS COMMUNISM?
1993, ISBN 0 7453 0806 6

3. WHAT WAS COMMUNISM? II
1993, ISBN 0 7453 0807 4

4. THE LABOUR PARTY SINCE 1945
1994, ISBN 0 7453 0808 2

5. THE LEFT AND CULTURE
1994, ISBN 0 7453 0809 0

6. THE PERSONAL AND THE POLITICAL
1994, ISBN 0 7453 0810 4

Editorial Team
Willie Thompson
David Parker
Mike Waite
David Morgan

Editorial Advisers
Noreen Branston
Rodney Hilton
Monty Johnstone
Victor Kiernan
Pat Thane
David Howell
Eric Hobsbawm

CONTENTS

Editorial
Willie Thompson   5

Part 1: The Second World War and After

The Journey to War
Raymond Challinor   13

Keeping the Home Fires Burning: the Albion Shop Stewards in the Second World War
Peter Bain and Tommy Gorman   27

The Second World War and Stalin
Dave Morgan   72

Part 2: Christianity and Socialism

The Grace of Alliance
Chris Bryant   79

Reviews   104

Nazism and German Society 1933–1945 edited David F Crew
Oded Heilbronner   104

The Politics of Continuity: British Foreign Policy and the Labour Government 1945–46 by John Saville
David Howell   106

The British New Left by Lin Chun
Stephen Woodhams   109

Witness Against the Beast: William Blake and the Moral Law by E P Thompson
V G Kiernan   116

The English Bible and the Seventeeth Century Revolution by Christopher Hill
Willie Thompson   119

Books Received   123
Information for Subscribers   126
Index   127

EDITORIAL

❏ Our new format

AT THE JANUARY 1995 AGM of the Socialist History Society it was agreed, following discussions between Pluto Press and the Society's committee, that *Socialist History* would benefit both editorially and financially from reorganisation in its appearance and structure.

Not that the format in which it has existed over the past two years has by any means been an unsuccessful one. It has been generally well received by readers, there has been a modest but encouraging rise in circulation and it has received commendations from respected historians. A number of the articles carried during that period have advanced knowledge and understanding significantly in the areas of socialist and labour history.

The disadvantage however, and principal frustration that we've always faced, has been the limitation on the size of individual issues of the journal, upon which a strict limit of 64 pages has had to be observed. This has meant restricting the length of particular articles to avoid unbalancing the issue in which they appear. Furthermore, contributors have had to wait sometimes excessive lengths of time for their material to appear because of the queue of articles and reviews building up.

The solution adopted is that the frequency of appearance of the journal will be reduced from three to two times a year, but that the individual issues will be much larger, so that overall there will be a considerably greater number of pages. The price for 1995 will remain the same: £15 for a year's subscription (£25 for Institutions) Individual numbers will be £7.95 each. Less *frequent* publication is of course always to be regretted, no matter how it is viewed and however great the compensating advantages, but Society members will benefit not only by having more journal in the course of a year but by receiving a free copy on one of the Society's occasional publications. In 1995 that will be the collection of tributes to the Marxist historian George Rudé.

Other beneficial aspects will also follow. The redesigned cover gives the journal a more striking appearance than before, and the larger size of each issue makes it attractive to bookshops. Every issue will continue to be structured around one or two themes. The current issue commemorates the 50th anniversary of the end of the Second

World War together with the consequent Labour victory of 1945, and its aftermath. The second theme treated in issue 7, not wholly unconnected, is the religious dimension in British radicalism. Issue 8, appearing in the autumn, will focus on historiography and the British Marxist historians, particularly Edward Thompson. Aspects of labour movements in Britain, Europe and the USA will feature in issue 9.

One less than satisfactory aspect of our publication in 1993 and 1994 has been that although three numbers appeared in both years, the dates of publication tended to be irregular, with lengthy gaps at the beginning of each year. We now hope to overcome this. From 1996 the months of publication will be March and September. This year, however, because the decision was arrived at only in January, the timing is of necessity somewhat later in the spring/summer and autumn/winter.

We are committed to continuing to provide a journal of the highest possible quality, both in content and presentation, that explores and assesses the socialist movement's past and the broader processes in relation to it, not only for the sake of historical understanding but as an input and contribution to its future development. The predecessor of today's journal, *Our History*, first appeared in October 1953 in the form of two sheets of foolscap stapled together, carrying an editorial and three brief articles. In one form or another, through many vicissitudes and changes of personnel, a continuous publication has been maintained since then. It seems worthwhile even now to quote a paragraph from that initial editorial – our basic aims nowadays are not all that different:

> [Articles] will all relate in some way or other to the historical development of the British people ... that is to say, they will be concerned with the kind of history that illuminates our own present struggles for a better life. This is intentionally broad, and no aspect of British history from which socialists can derive some new understanding, or inspiration, will be excluded.
>
> In the second place, the articles will normally include unpublished material or will attempt a new approach to the subject, and will therefore have some historical value in themselves.
>
> This bulletin will be duplicated at present. But our ultimate aim is a printed magazine ... (!)

❑ Issue 7: Fighting the Good Fight?

The Second World War

The years between 1939 and the early 1950s constituted the most profound and extensive cataclysm of modern times, if not indeed in the entire historical record. In the world conflict at least 50 million people lost their lives, the majority of them non-combatants. The scale of destruction of material values was incalculable. For the first time since the medieval era the administrative structures of major states were utterly annihilated and every surviving artefact of their regimes, down to their archives and their art collections, removed to foreign capitals. The ultimate weapon, employing the uncontrolled release of nuclear energy, made its appearance and was tested on human populations.

In the aftermath, political and social revolution swept the globe; mighty empires, recently victorious in the titanic struggle, crumbled irreversibly. The United States ascended to economic, political and military hegemony over all societies adhering to the institutions of private property and market systems, while the USSR assumed the (temporary) leadership of those who rejected them. The life-and-death combat of Allies and Axis was succeeded by a bipolar standoff between superpowers representing antagonistic social orders, threatening each other (and everybody else) with nuclear armageddon.

Out of these cataclysms the contemporary world was born. The Second World War and its aftermath comprehensively obliterated the international social, economic and political order that the previous global conflict had fractured but still left standing. Out of what conditions then did the war itself arise?

Roots of the catastrophe
By the beginning of the twentieth century the world processes of industrialisation and technological enhancement, proceeding for over a hundred years, had generated an infinitely complex network of commodity interchange and financial circuits. Its political form took the shape of world empires in economic, diplomatic and military competition, one of which, the British, though faltering in technological competitiveness, dominated with ease the global communication and financial networks.

Between 1914 and 1918 the unstable equilibrium underwent bloody disruption as the ascendant German empire pursued a strenuous challenge for global hegemony against the ageing British rival. Lenin's characterisation of the conflict as a war for the redivision of imperialist plunder, though oversimplified and mistaken in detail, is accurate in essence. At its conclusion the chief combatants, having exhausted themselves and in the process torn apart the fabric of international exchange, left the way open for the USA to emerge as Britain's successor to dominion over the world economy. The other principal transformation in the world order produced by the first war was the revolutionary irruption of the Soviet state, a terrifying menace to the bourgeois order everywhere because of its size, its example and its initial promotion of world revolution.

Bolshevism was one novel form of postwar politics: another was fascism. During the 1920s it was largely confined to Italy, with local outgrowths in Germany and Austria, but following the deepening of the world slump between 1929 and 1932 it appeared in every European country.

There is no historical consensus on either exactly what fascism was or on the reasons for the peculiarly horrendous dynamism of its German variant, but the broad outlines are clear enough. In every instance it began as a mobilisation of lower middle-class groups and individuals experiencing threats to their property, incomes and status. Terrified equally by the prospect of being sacrificed to the necessities of big capital in trouble and by that of socialist revolution, they committed themselves to authoritarian and violent responses. They purported to be revolutionaries, partly in hope of stealing support from the left and partly because the word had positive connotations, implying the overthrow of corrupt and decrepit structures, but they were 'revolutionaries' in defence of property and of 'law and order'. On that basis they were able, in countries where they succeeded in becoming a substantial political force, to forge an alliance with traditional and propertied elites, aiming together at extirpating the left, liquidating class struggle and reviving national splendour.

In only two such regimes however did the fascist party emerge as the senior partner in this kind of coalition, with its leader as the charismatic national dictator, namely Italy and Germany. Eric Hobsbawm notes in *Age of Extremes* that if the Italian variety had been the only sort of fascism on offer, the ruling elites of interwar France and Britain would have accommodated themselves to it willingly enough – they certainly tried their hardest to accommodate even to the Hitlerian version, which was of a distinctly different metal. In the end they could not do so because the Third Reich undertook to resume the purposes of its Wilhelmine predecessor and bid for world hegemony. The first phase of the project was intended to be the conquest, subjugation and enslavement of Eastern Europe, and while the leaders of the Western democracies were perfectly happy to bargain with Hitler over this, they could not, at the expense of their own interests and credibility, offer him the unlimited 'free hand' that he demanded. Once the Nazi armies in 1940 had subjugated Western Europe the war developed from being one of comparatively limited aims and operations to one of all-out struggle for survival, the more so following the assault on the USSR in June 1941 and the opening of the Pacific war in December of the same year.

Nazi imperatives
There can be no serious doubt that the responsibility for unleashing the war, and then extending its scope – against the almost unanimous advice of his hierarchs – lay with one individual. The important question however is not one of Adolf Hitler's personality, but the expectations and judgements which caused him to act in such a manner. He was of course a monomaniacal racist and imperialist, a psychopathic gangster, convinced that Germany's immediate destiny lay in the construction of a vast slave empire in Eastern Europe – but his career up to 1939 also demonstrated that he was no fool. In point of fact his criminal ambitions in the later 1930s exactly coincided with the economic necessities of the Third Reich – a regime founded upon a historic compromise and division of labour between German capital and traditional elites on the one hand and Nazi political adventurers on the other.

Hitler's regime had succeeded in accomplishing an apparent economic miracle, pulling the country out of the depths of slump, bringing industry to full capacity working and eliminating unemployment, while by means of rigid wage controls restoring profitability as well, all upon the basis of a sort of militarised Keynesianism. However the undertaking was not without cost, and by the end of the decade the German economy was in deep trouble, with a catastrophic balance of payments deficit, government borrowing running out of control, looming inflation, and wage costs threatening to erupt as employers found ways around state controls in order to bid against each other for scarce labour. The regime – and Hitler was perfectly frank about this – was not willing to risk social discontent by forcing down consumption, even if the Gestapo saw to it that the discontent remained passive rather than active. The only other alternative was to amass fresh supplies of cheap land, labour and raw materials – which meant territorial expansionism. As early as November 1937 Hitler had outlined to his chiefs – including the non-Nazis who headed the economy, the armed forces and the diplomatic service – the initial stages of what he proposed to do, holding back on the greater projects because of expected opposition. However even the risks of annexing Austria and Czechoslovakia so terrified the conservatives that early the following year they were removed from their posts and replaced with more acquiescent subordinates.

The aftermath and the British role
And so the countdown started. The scope of the ensuing conflict however, together with its politicisation – the understanding that the war was as much a contestation of ideologies as of states – ensured that its consequences escaped from the control of even the victorious capitalist powers who, in the aftermath, found their imperial hegemony challenged all over the world by populations who had absorbed the anti-Axis message of national independence and human rights. The weaker imperial powers, with their own economies desperately fragile and facing internal social upheaval, implored the enormously-strengthened USA for material, moral and military support.

The British state and its people were at the heart of both the wartime inferno and the new chapter of global political relationships. The desperate emergency of the conflict, when the country for a time stood in imminent danger of invasion and conquest had, even in advance of peacetime reconstruction, led to its economy becoming structurally reliant on US resources and support. With the discredit of the prewar conservative leaders who had brought on the catastrophe, and the imperative need for national solidarity and commitment, it also resulted in a widespread determination to rebuild the nation as a community of welfare and social justice. Significant steps in that direction were implemented under the Churchill coalition, even while the war was still in progress, and taken seriously in hand with the Labour Party's landslide election victory in 1945.

The record of the Attlee government which took office in July 1945 remains an area of intense historical – and political – debate. On the right it is indicted for removing 20 per cent of the national economy out of private ownership and diverting national resources into excessive programmes of social welfare – an enervating 'new Jerusalem' – rather than market-led economic renewal. The left's critique focuses on the ultimately futile determination at all costs to retain the status of a world Great Power whatever the cost to the foundations of the nation's economy, the welfare of its people or the risks of thermo-nuclear annihilation. At the same time, the very real achievements of this government, attained in the face of immeasurably difficult circumstances, would be denied by few observers on the left – although they might question their scope and implementation. We have perhaps only really begun to appreciate their merits since their dismantling in the past 15 years.

Socialism and Christianity

If these advances marked the high tide of labourism, then without any doubt one of the principal strands in that form of social democracy has been the tradition of Christian socialism, which originated in Britain and has informed the development of this country's labour movement more than any of its counterparts. Indeed, few members of Attlee's government would have repudiated the connection.

The articles and reviews

All of these themes are addressed from a variety of angles in the current issue of the journal. Raymond Challinor presents an interpretation of the diplomatic manoeuvres leading up to the war and Dave Morgan assesses its course and outcome. It is expected that most readers of *Socialist History* will find both pieces controversial, in line with the journal's policy of stimulating historical debate. The centrepiece on this theme is a lengthy article by Tom Gorman and Peter Bain dealing with the impact of the war on the industrial workforce in the west of Scotland, as reflected in developments within a particular Glasgow factory. What is most invaluable and enlightening here and constitutes a significant contribution to our understanding, are both the similarities and contrasts with the era of the 'Red Clyde' during the First World War.

In the reviews relating to this theme, Oded Heilbronner covers an important recent text concerning the nature of German society under the Nazis. John Saville's recent research has done a great deal to fill in the picture of the 1945–51 Labour government's foreign policies, and his book on that subject is reviewed here by David Howell. In the long perspective, it was the shortcomings of both labourism and orthodox communism which led to the emergence of the New Left in Britain during the later 1950s. Historical attention is now starting to be focused on this movement, and Stephen Woodhams reviews one of the resulting books.

The background and meaning of Christian socialism is comprehensively covered by Chris Bryant and reviews relating to texts concerned with religion and radical politics are reviewed respectively by Victor Kiernan and the editor. Readers will be particularly interested in Victor's sympathetic but not uncritical handling of the exploration by E P Thompson of the difficult and obscure but highly suggestive writings and thought of William Blake, his 'very individual interpretation of Christianity'.

Finally, a number of important historical conferences are taking place in the course of 1995. We hope to carry brief reports in subsequent numbers. *Socialist History* is still looking for participants in its enterprise, whether as contributors or in other capacities. Any interested reader should get in touch with the editor.

Willie Thompson

Apology

To Yvonne Kapp. The reference on p. 19 of *Socialist History* 6 should have been to the *Berlin* Institute of Marxism-Leninism. 'Berlin' was omitted from the printed text of her article.

The Editors

Part One: The Second World War and After
THE JOURNEY TO WAR

Raymond Challinor

THE BRITISH LEFT FACED the prospect of a second world war with dark fatalism and fear. A typical reaction came in 1934 from Ellen Wilkinson and Dr Edward Conze, a refugee from fascism, then her partner. Together they wrote a booklet, its title reveals a certain resignation, *Why War ? A Handbook for those who will take part in the Second World War*. Participants in the impending conflict were even left a few empty pages at the end, where they could scribble a few notes about the struggle. Equally certain that conflict lay ahead was F A Ridley. Slightly prematurely, he called his book, published in 1936, *Next Year's War*.[1]

Besides making virtually the same analysis, F A Ridley and Ellen Wilkinson had something else in common. When Leon Trotsky sent an American Trotskyist, Max Shachtman as his emissary to London – his purpose being to form a revolutionary organisation in Britain – both their names were on his recruitment list. But neither joined the small group formed by Reg Groves and Harry Wicks.[2]

Yet, whatever their disagreement with Trotsky, they remained in fundamental agreement with him on the crucial issue of war. All of them believed it remained an inherent feature of capitalism, one of its contradictions that would tend to worsen and become more destructive over time. Unless an international socialist society were created, Trotsky forecast that the world would plunge into barbarism – what Marx in *The Communist Manifesto* had termed 'the general ruin of the contending classes'. The orgies of self-destruction would extinguish humanity; the planet would be left to other species, like the happy amoeba and the contented swine, sufficiently intelligent not to indulge in periodic attempts to commit collective suicide.[3]

Powerful forces operated in society that were beyond control of the capitalists themselves. Businessmen wished to produce profits. None of them wished to make losses or to go bankrupt and fling themselves off tall buildings because they were completely ruined. Yet, quite independent of their volition, from time to time, their system plunges them into slumps. Similarly, wars arise not because of the wickedness of a particular individual; rather the desperate problems, created by international competition, could not be resolved in any other way.

❏ Leninism and the War

In his book *Imperialism*, Lenin enunciated what he saw as the basic causes of capitalist war. All developed, industrialised countries were driven by the same imperatives. They needed to dominate, better still rule, places where opportunities for highly profitable investment existed. Associated with this, they needed to control sources of raw materials, necessary for their security and well-being. If a plentiful supply of cheap labour were available, then this was a further bonus. As imperial possessions were so profitable, every advanced capitalist country sought to grab them. After a while the problem was that, with all such territories taken, one country could only expand its empire at the expense of another. This, from Lenin's viewpoint, provided the underlying tensions which caused the First World War.

The revolutionary left argued that all these influences mentioned by Lenin continued to operate in the period before the Second World War but were augmented by other potent forces. To pull themselves out from the slump of 1929–31, the most severe ever experienced by capitalism, the major capitalist countries turned to economic nationalism. Imperial preference, quotas, tariff barriers and barter agreements helped to provide a modicum of national security to the homebased industries. However, a semblance of economic security was gained at the cost of political insecurity. A country like Britain, safe behind the barriers it had erected, inevitably generated frustration from countries like Germany, with more dynamic economies, afraid these might explode unless new export markets were found. Slogans like 'Export or die' (in other words, a nation's economic survival depended upon capturing foreign markets) or 'Guns or butter' (with its barely hidden assumption that military means would be the ultimate arbiter) expressed the growing feeling of lethal desperation.

Trotsky saw the crisis in the following way:

> The flagrant and ever-growing disproportion between the specific weight of France and England, not to mention Holland, Belgium and Portugal, in the world economy, and the colossal dimensions of their colonial possessions are as much the source of world conflicts and of new wars as the insatiable greed of the fascist 'aggressors'. To put it better, the two phenomena are but two sides of the same coin. The 'peaceful' British and French democracies rest on the suppression of national democratic movements of hundreds of millions in Asia and Africa for the sake of the super-

profits derived from them. Conversely, Hitler and Mussolini promise to become more 'moderate' if they obtain adequate colonial territory.[4]

The Treaty of Versailles, no longer corresponding to the respective countries' economic strengths, seemed ready to buckle and break under increasing strain. How were the drastic changes to be made? The re-armament that took place in most advanced countries provided the answer.

But as socialist economists pointed out, re-armament posed dangerous difficulties for Britain. Margaret Laws, writing in *Controversy*, dwelt on the UK's economic decline and its lost markets. To divert production from exports to armaments would hasten this process of loss. So military strength could be gained through increasing economic weakness, a loss of markets that would never be reconquered.[5]

❏ Government perceptions

Although Margaret Laws was obviously not privy to the discussions privately held by the British cabinet, her thoughts – and those of other socialists – roughly corresponded with those expressed behind closed doors by many of the top people. In 1931, the British cabinet had been told by the chiefs of staff that growing Japanese might threatened British possessions in the Far East: 'The position is about as bad as it could be', the *Imperial Defence Review* of 1932 stated, 'the whole of our territory in the Far East, as well as the coastline of India and the Dominions and our vast trade and shipping, lies open to attack'.[6] A few years later it heard the same dire warnings about Italy: Britain did not possess the military might to contain any threat from Mussolini in the Mediterranean. Then, again, after Munich, Sir Alexander Cadogan told the Cabinet that Britain did not have the power to thwart German expansionism: 'I believe that any deliberate uneconomic "encirclement" of Germany will be futile and ruinous'. He advocated: 'let Germany, if she can, find her "Lebensraum" and establish herself'.[7]

In view of such weakness, it could be thought, government advisers might have advocated drastic re-armament. Far from it. Besides the three arms of His Majesty's Forces, Sir Thomas Inskip told the ministers to protect 'the fourth arm of defence' – the country's economic strength. If that were undermined, Britain would be defenceless. A sound economy underpinned everything else, and this would be jeopardised by all-out re-armament. Britain's weak economy would sink beneath the weight of military hardware.

One of the heads of British intelligence, Major Whitehead, warned ministers that a 'life and death struggle with Germany would bring ruination'. He thought that Britain would be well-advised to try and steer Germany in an easterly direction. Hitler's *Dracht nacht Osten*, his drive to the East, would eventually bring him bumping up against the Soviet Union: 'From a conflict between Germany and Russia, which would probably ruin our two potential enemies in Europe, we have little to lose, and might even gain considerably'.[8]

Though not privy to such secret state papers, the left sensed the big powers sparred with each other in a murky underworld of power politics. An editorial in the *New International* declared in May 1939:

> If two clever gangsters should be getting ready to fight each other, and if they wished to win public support for their respective sides, each of them could make out a plausible case. All that each would have to do, in speeches and appeals, would be to concentrate all emphasis on the crimes of the other, and let the positive argument rest on vague and noble generalities that could never be pinned down.
>
> Imperialist gangsters differ chiefly in scale from the Capones and Torrios.[9]

As more documents of the various nations become accessible, the truth of the *New International* comparison acquires still greater weight. Every government resorted to crime, deception and double-dealing. Simultaneous protestations of love and peace towards another country would be accompanied by hidden plans for war against it. This kind of conduct was akin to that practised in Renaissance Italy at the time of Machiavelli, when 'friendly' pats on the back of one diplomat by another were banned – beneath the long-flowing cloaks daggers might be concealed.

❑ The USSR and the West

With the war approaching, Britain's policy provides a good illustration of realpolitik in operation. Seeking to lay plans for every eventuality, Chamberlain and his cabinet realised that a war with Germany was a possibility. In such circumstances, the hands of Britain and France would be strengthened if the Soviet Union could be

THE JOURNEY TO WAR

inveigled into becoming an ally. But there were grave doubts about the Soviet Union. A backward and undeveloped country, it might quickly be crushed by an onslaught of modern armies. Moreover, Stalin had recently unleashed waves of purges. Among the many talented people he murdered were Marshal Tuchachevsky, the head of the Red Army, and many other high-ranking officers. Just as the slaying of the manager and many of the star players of a football team might place a question mark over its ability to win the world cup, so doubts existed that Soviet forces, poorly equipped and poorly led, would be able to acquit themselves well.

Even so, the British and French governments thought that no avenue should be left unexplored. Consequently, in the summer of 1939, each government dispatched a representative for negotiations in Moscow. Dawdling along in a slow boat to Leningrad, their laid-back approach probably gave the Soviet leaders the feeling that the two governments attached little importance or urgency to the mission. Once they arrived in the Kremlin, they followed normal diplomatic procedure and gave their names in full.

This caused quite a stir as Britain's representative had the longest ever known surname. Soviet statesmen sat bewildered as he told them he was none other than Admiral Sir Reginald Aylmer Ranfurty Plunket-ErnleErle-Drax-Drax. He went on to regale them with a list of his various honours and had just reached the Order of the Bath, when one of the Russians politely inquired why the Order had gained such a peculiar title. Alas, the noble admiral did not know. On the spur of the moment he invented a story: in the Middle Ages the monarchs and their nobles enjoyed hunting. This made them dirty, and therefore afterwards they needed a wash. On hearing this explanation, the Soviet delegation fell about in laughter, presumably muttering to one another, 'It's a right one they have sent us here, tovarish'.[10]

But there were other, much more serious, reasons why the mission failed. The Soviet statesmen thought that Britain and France could not be trusted. While they would receive with alacrity Russian support if they were attacked, they would not so enthusiastically meet their obligations and come to Russia's aid if she were attacked. Already the Kremlin knew of manifest Anglo-French hostility dating back to the Churchill-led expeditionary force that invaded Russia in 1919. Numerous other attempts at sabotage and spying came in later years. As they were negotiating in 1939, a further plot was being hatched: Fitzroy Maclean, a Foreign Office agent and later Tory MP for Lancaster, thought the ethnic and religious unrest in Soviet Central Asia provided the opportunity to undermine Moscow control. He sought to infiltrate into the region Afghans and Iranians – looking for all intent and purpose like Soviet subjects, but loyal to Britain – to fan the flames of disaffection. More recently, the *Independent* has published details of Fitzroy Maclean's work under the headline: 'A 1939 Foreign Office memo saw upheaval in Central Asia as Stalin's Achilles' heel: British "plot" aimed to destabilise Soviets.'[11]

Another Anglo-French plan, designed to cripple the Soviet economy by bombing the Caucasus oilfields and so depriving it of fuel, was also devised in 1939. The RAF aircraft undertaking the photographic reconnaissance of the Baku encountered Russian anti-aircraft fire. These plans were frequently updated and when the Wehrmacht captured Paris in the summer of 1940, the most recently revised plans were discovered in the French Foreign Office. As the Soviet Union was then Germany's ally – the Rippentrop–Molotov pact had been signed – the Nazis passed on the plans to Moscow as a friendly gesture. Still the matter remained a serious proposition: amazingly as late as 31 May 1941, when Germany controlled the Continent and Britain stood alone, the military leaders in London still found time to contemplate bombing the Caucasus oilfields.[12]

❑ **Barbarossa**

What makes it intriguing is that 31 May is only three weeks before 22 June 1941, the day Hitler launched Barbarossa against the Soviet Union, the biggest ever military offensive in human history. Incontestable evidence exists that Britain, for many months, had known about Hitler's plans and warned the Kremlin of the impending attack. The compelling question remains: did some in high places want to see the invasion to be a joint German–British venture? As it was, German troops came close to defeating the Soviet Union. Had Britain thrown in its armed forces, too, it might have tipped the balance. Together, by their joint efforts, Britain and Germany may have won the huge, and largely untapped, resource of the Soviet Union, a vast new area to exploit.

Clearly, Stalin feared a combined Anglo-German onslaught might be contemplated. Maxim Litvinov, the Soviet ambassador in Washington later confided to Joseph E Davies, an American friend

THE JOURNEY TO WAR

of Stalinism, who had written *Mission to Moscow*, a sympathetic account of Soviet foreign policy: 'All [the Russian leaders] believed that the British fleet was steaming up the North Sea for a joint attack with Hitler on Leningrad and Kronstadt'.[13]

The suspicions of Stalin must have been heightened by a mysterious event that had occurred a few days before. On 10 May 1941 Rudolf Hess, Hitler's deputy, had flown to Britain. The reasons behind this dramatic move have never been revealed. The Public Records Office still keep some documents secret; others, according to Alan Clark, the military historian and former Minister of Defence, have been deliberately destroyed. He considers the authorities would find the revelations they contain too embarrassing: Hess, it seems, had come to negotiate peace between Britain and Germany. Whether he also wanted British participation in the attack on Russia remains unclear. That the events of 10 May 1941 and 22 June 1941 were closely linked remained a conviction widely held. Immediately after the German offensive began a spokesman for the British Communist Party declared it was 'the sequel of the secret moves which have been taking place behind the curtain of the Hess mission'.[14]

Russian leaders would be mindful that little more than a year before, Anglo-French and German forces came close to fighting against the Soviet Union. This occurred in the final phase of the Soviet Union's war against Finland. In October 1939, Stalin attacked the Finns from a mixture of imperialist and defensive reasons. Obviously he wished to enhance the USSR's power and wealth by incorporating Finland. Yet, also, he was aware of how the existing Finnish frontiers placed the Soviet Union in a dangerous military position. When he built St Petersburg, Peter the Great called it Russia's window on Europe. What he perhaps could have added was that the Finnish-owned Åland islands, strategically situated in the Baltic, constituted the shutters that could at any time be used to block off the window. Moreover, the Russo-Finnish frontier then ran precariously near to Leningrad, Russia's second city, putting it within easy shelling distance. This was made more menacing because many of the big powers, potential enemies of the Soviet Union, had for years helped to build up Finland's military. And this is what happened during the winter war: supplies came from Britain, France and Germany. As Finland's position deteriorated, these countries decided to stiffen resistance by sending their own troops to fight alongside the Finns. On 5 February 1940, the Allied Supreme War Council decided to dispatch six British divisions and 50,000 French troops. Three hundred British volunteers, presumably the precursors of the present-day SAS, had already arrived in Helsinki. The prospect of Anglo-French troops fighting alongside German ones was only thwarted because Finland sued for peace on 29 February 1940.

❏ Anglo–US rivalry

If it was not inconceivable to find British and French troops fighting alongside their German counterparts, then there is another scenario that has been discreetly forgotten: Anglo-French hostility towards the United States. Though it may seem strange today, American military manoeuvres in the 1920s were held on the supposition that America was being invaded by British troops stationed in Canada. In 1929, the US government drew up top secret plans for war with Britain, aimed at driving the British from both North and South America. This fear of an Anglo-American war may have receded slightly in the 1930s. Even so, sources of tension still remained, particularly in the Pacific and Latin America. On 17 March 1939, two events happened: first, German troops marched into Prague; and, second, this violation of the recently-signed Munich agreement did not prevent the Dusseldorf accords between the Federation of British Industry and Reichsgruppe Industrie, its German equivalent, being signed. Their objective was to strengthen Anglo-German economic cooperation, thereby enhancing their mutual competitive position throughout the world.

Both the prime minister, Neville Chamberlain, and Oliver Stanley, president of the Board of Trade, publicly welcomed the agreement. In May 1939, they agreed to the Bank of International Settlement sending $25 million worth of Czech gold from London to Berlin. Two British government advisers, Robert Hudson and Sir Horace Wilson negotiated with their Nazi counterparts the possibility of a $5,000 million loan to the Third Reich. The British ambassador to Germany, Sir Neville Henderson, stated these were all signs of Britain offering the hand of friendship to Germany.[16]

As the British political left recognised, the Dusseldorf accords and other measures were designed primarily as an anti-American move. Cooperation, it was hoped, would halt the United States economic advance in Latin America. Hopefully, together they would be able to stop the erosion of British influence there while simultaneously

THE JOURNEY TO WAR

helping Germany successfully to counter the growing Yankee dominance of the continent. United they would stand; divided they would fall to the Dollar.

Old habits die hard, as do old antipathies. Even when, in the 1940s, Britain and Germany had been foes for years, a lot of influential Americans found it difficult to recognise the changed relationship. In his history of the OSS, the forerunner of the CIA, Professor R Harris Smith plainly admitted: 'Many OSS men began to operate on the general principle that the British are just as much the enemy as the Germans. They believed that London's secret services were more concerned with expanding England's empire than with defeating the enemy'.[17]

Yet US foreign policy appears to have been equally prefaced by considerations of self-interest. Up to Munich in 1938, it strove to maintain peace. Soviet historians suggest this was done because any war would be of short duration, affording the United States little opportunity to expand exports to either belligerent. However, as it became likely any conflict would be both prolonged and of great severity, American foreign policy changed. It threatened that, unless Britain and France stood up to German expansionism, their supplies of vital raw material supplies would be cut off. Joseph P Kennedy, American ambassador in London, said that 'neither the French nor the British would have made Poland a cause of war if it had not been for the constant needling from Washington. ... In the summer of 1939, the President kept telling him (Kennedy) to put some iron up Chamberlain's backside'.[18]

But there was more than a hint of American double-dealing and double-crossing. In early October 1939, President Roosevelt sent a personal envoy to Berlin in the shape of William Rhodes Davis, an influential oil tycoon. In the discussion, Davis assured the Nazi leaders that Roosevelt's main strategic concern was to destroy Britain's position in world markets. The President wished to know Germany's terms for a peace settlement. He would then bring pressure for British and French compliance. Were they to fail to do so, then the United States would supply Germany with goods and war material 'convoyed to Germany under the protection of the American armed forces'.[19]

❑ Strategy and diplomacy

It may appear difficult to disentangle from the myriad of plots and counter-plots, deceptions and subterfuges, indulged in by the major powers how any country determined its foreign policy. Doubtless, a considerable amount of uncertainty prevailed, with contingency plans for fighting a large number of possible enemies. Equally, possible allies were also as numerous. In these circumstances, it seems hardly surprising that Trotsky, a perceptive observer of international affairs in 1938, predicted that a war would occur but was unwilling to forecast the line-up of protagonists.

Nevertheless, a useful clue to what the crucial domestic influences were that helped to determine British foreign policy may come unwittingly from a well-known remark of Chamberlain, made soon after Munich. He described Czechoslovakia as a far away country about which most people knew nothing. This was probably true of 80 per cent of the British population. In those days communications were not as highly developed as they are today; few Britons would have ever met a Czech and most would not be unduly perturbed about its fate. But who would be concerned? Certainly businessmen, financiers and traders who had economic links with Czechoslovakia would be concerned with whether they could continue, perhaps expand, their operations; with the social climate of a country in which they functioned; and whether the political structure was congenial and provided security. So it would be these capitalist interests that would have a definite opinion of what should be done, whether there should be peace or war. The input to the decision-making process of the working class, usually limited on home affairs, would be all the more limited on foreign issues.

Of course, whatever decision was taken would have its impact elsewhere. Britain's failure to resist German encroachments in Czechoslovakia sent a shiver of insecurity to those with economic ties in the Balkans and even into the Middle East. Britain's subsequent decision, however, to go to war over the invasion of Poland would have exactly the opposite repercussions. With the country's resources committed to war against Germany, the already inadequate cover provided elsewhere would be weakened still further. While Britain was preoccupied, America, Italy, Japan and Russia would feel under less restraint to respect British interests. (By British interests, of course, we always mean British *capitalist* interests; workers would merely act as spectators.)

Consequently diplomacy is like an iceberg, with five-sixths hidden from view. Most of the lobbying and negotiating is conducted informally in secret. It remains, nevertheless, effective. The human

THE JOURNEY TO WAR

moneybags get their way silently, without the public even hearing the clink of coinage. Similarly, with peace discussions: in neutral countries – Sweden or Spain for example – businessmen from many nations use the same restaurants. Friend and foe may meet over a drink and exchange views. In such circumstances, the respective embassies can ask their businessmen to float a proposal. Should it prove fruitful, it can then later be taken up through official channels. Should it prove an embarrassment, it can simply be disowned.

During the Second World War, the influence of the wealthy on the decision-making process happened in every country. As we have seen, the oil magnate, William Rhodes Davis, was Roosevelt's emissary at the beginning of the conflict. In the final phase, Myrom Taylor, the tough leader of the American steel bosses, helped to secure a peace favourable to US interests. Then between big business and the intelligence services there was much intermeshing. One of America's wealthiest men, Andrew Mellon's son Paul, was at OSS's Special Operations Branch in London. His sister Ailsa, one of the world's richest women, was married to David Bruce, head of OSS operations in London. He was the son of a senator and a millionaire in his own right. Other Mellons and Mellons-in-Law held OSS positions in Madrid, Geneva and Paris. And so one could go on.[20]

❑ Appeasers

Of course, in Britain, Chamberlain's government represented capitalist interests. Where divisions existed on a foreign policy issue, then usually no inhibitions were felt about battling for one's corner. In her famous book about Jarrow, Ellen Wilkinson does not suggest it met a natural death. Her title was not *The Town that Died* but *The Town that Was Murdered* – and murder involves a deliberate, conscious act. She explained how a British and German shipbuilders' cartel sought to restrict production so profits could be increased. The slaughter of Jarrow shipyard was the consequence. Because of the mutually advantageous arrangements, many industrialists did not want Britain to go to war with Germany. Six of their representatives conducted secret negotiations in an attempt to avert the conflict. Those involved in this move were: Sir Charles Maclaren, of Thomas Brown (shipbuilder), S W Dawson of Thomas Forth (steel manufacturer), Sir Robert Renwick of London Electrical Supply, Brian S Mountain of Eagle Star (investment and insurance), Frederick Spicer of Thomas Brown and T Mensforth of Hotpoint (electrical manufacturer). At the Nuremberg war crimes trial in 1946, Hermann Goering commended their efforts to secure peace.

But the supreme Nazi accolade went to Lord Londonderry, former treasurer of the Conservative Party and County Durham's biggest coalowner. In 1938, Penguin published his book *Ourselves and Germany*. The blurb stated: 'It is the clearest exposition so far of the policy of rapprochement with Nazi Germany and for a more sympathetic [approach to] Herr Hitler's point of view. Few men have played such an important part in our diplomatic relations with Germany as Lord Londonderry. During his frequent visits abroad he spent considerable time with Hitler, Goering, Neurath and Ribbentrop'. As if to underline the prevailing spirit of goodwill, the book finishes with letters commending the work from Field Marshal Goering, Franz von Papen, Joachim Stresemann and the Bishop of Durham. However, the first letter, saying how much he has enjoyed reading the book and appreciates His Lordship's efforts to promote Anglo-German understanding, ends: 'With my best wishes to Lady Londonderry and with friendly greetings, Yours cordially, Adolf Hitler'. In the circumstances, was it surprising that an Anglo-German coal agreement was signed in January 1939 – two months before the Dusseldorf accords?

Besides those wanting Anglo-German cooperation because, when two are shaking the tree's branches more plums are likely to drop off than if one was doing it alone, there was another group with slightly different interests that wanted to promote better relations between Britain and Germany. The multi-national firm Unilever felt war would disrupt its business. This probably prompted four of its directors to sit on the governing body of the Anglo-German Friendship Society. Though powerful influences were operating to stop war with Germany, government ministers had to decide from where weak and ailing Britain was menaced the most. To put all its efforts into a life-and-death struggle with country A necessarily meant that the already inadequate resources to protect British interests against countries B, C and D would be further depleted. Consequently, war against one nation, even if it ended in victory, would mean silently enduring losses inflicted by others. A balance sheet has two sides. Arriving at a decision about who to fight involved an agonising process. It was only resolved in August 1939 by the Molotov–Ribbentrop pact. The agreement reached between Germany and the Soviet Union represented a threat to British interests throughout the world, a threat that far exceeded gains that British firms might hope to accrue from possible Anglo-German cooperation.

For centuries, Britain had fought to maintain a balance of power in Europe, preventing any one state from achieving dominance. Clearly, the combined strength of Germany and Russia would make them supreme. Together, controlling a vast land-mass, stretching from Europe to the Middle East and the Pacific Ocean, virtually the entire British Empire would be under threat and, finally, against the twoheaded monster even the nation would be imperilled. So reluctantly, on 3 September 1939, Neville Chamberlain, the British prime minister, declared war.

NOTES

1. Ellen Wilkinson and Dr Edward Conze, *Why War?* (National Council of Labour Colleges, 1934) and F A Ridley, *Next Year's War?* (Secker and Warburg, 1936).
2. Martin Richard Upham, The History of British Trotskyism to 1949 (PhD, Hull University, 1980), p. 32.
3. Leon Trotsky, *Marxism in Our Time* (Pathfinder Press, 1970), pp. 46–7.
4. Leon Trotsky, *Writings 1938–9* (Pathfinder Press, 1969), p. 54.
5. *Controversy*, April 1939.
6. Chief of Staff 295, Imperial Defence Policy, 23 February 1932. Cab.53/22.
7. Cadogan memo, 14 October 1938, quoted in David Dilks (ed), *Diaries of Sir Alexander Cadogan 1938–45* (Cassells, 1971), pp. 116–20.
8. Cabinet Papers 316(37), 15 December 1937. Cab.24/273.
9. *New International*, May 1939.
10. D C Watt, *How War Came* (Mandarin, 1989), pp. 452–4.
11. *Independent*, 26 February 1990; Foreign Office File 57364. Now not open to public inspection until 2015. Ironically, at the Lancaster byelection in October 1941, the Communist Party were among Fitzroy-Maclean's most enthusiastic supporters. They broke up an ILP election meeting and went off shouting 'A vote for Brockway is a vote for Hitler'.
12. Gabriel Gorodetsky, *Stafford Cripps' Mission to Moscow 1940–42* (Gollancz, 1942), pp. 24, 54, 104 and 143.
13. J E Davies papers, box 11 (Library of Congress). Also Lord Halifax papers A.7.8.9, diary 11 December 1941.
14. *Daily Express*, 23 June 1941.
15. Neville Chamberlain, House of Commons, 19 March 1940.

16. D F Fleming, *The Cold War and its origins 1917–60* (Allen and Unwin, 1961), vol.I, p. 92.

17. Peter Tompkins, *Italy Betrayed* (Simon and Schuster, 1966), p. 253, and R Harris Smith, *OSS: The Secret History of America's First Central Intelligence Agency* (University of California Press, 1972) p. 34.

18. Charles C Tansill, *Back Door to War: The Roosevelt Foreign Policy*, (Chicago, 1952) p. 555.

19. David Irving, *The War Path: Hitler's Germany 1933–1939* (Macmillan, 1973), p. 32.

20. R Harris Smith, *OSS*, pp. 15–16.

Raymond Challinor formerly taught at Newcastle Polytechnic. He has written widely on British socialist history.

KEEPING THE HOME FIRES BURNING: THE ALBION SHOP STEWARDS IN THE SECOND WORLD WAR

Peter Bain and Tommy Gorman

IN THE TWENTIETH CENTURY, the ability of a nation-state's engineering industry to produce sufficient quantities of weapons, munitions and transport has proved a crucial factor whenever competition on the economic front has exploded into all-out military conflict. When Britain entered the Second World War in September 1939, memories of the widespread industrial unrest generated by the unofficial shop stewards movement only 20–25 years earlier was still fresh in the minds of employers and government.[1]

Nowhere was this unease felt more acutely than with regard to the situation on Clydeside, for it was there that the Clyde Workers Committee (CWC) had been born in 1915, the forerunner of similar rank-and-file bodies in all the main engineering centres.[2] The Workers Committees were able to lead unofficial (and illegal) strikes of up to 250,000 engineering workers and, at times, the movement's socialist leadership had seemed close to fusing shopfloor discontent over wartime working conditions with opposition to the war itself. The CWC's last effective intervention took place in the strike for the 40-hour week in 1919, when heavily armed troops occupied Glasgow and Britain's rulers contemplated the possibility of working-class insurrection. However, the Workers Committee movement was effectively crushed by the massive wave of redundancies and victimisations in the engineering industry in the early 1920s. In the military conflict which Britain entered in 1939, the massive heavy engineering and shipbuilding complex centred upon Glasgow would again be of crucial importance to the war effort. From the point of view of both captains of industry and government ministers, a repetition of the events of 1915–19 had to be avoided.

As those charged with the responsibility for overseeing and organising Britain's war production surveyed the industrial relations landscape in 1939, they might have feared storm clouds lay ahead. Many of the leading shop stewards in the Workers Committees had joined the Communist Party when it was founded in 1920, and Clydeside had always been one of the Party's strongest areas, both numerically and in terms of influence on the shopfloor. Furthermore, as the British economy – stimulated by arms-spending – slowly recovered after the 1929–33 depression, there was clear evidence that the Communist Party had succeeded in gaining a strong foothold in the new metal industries (e.g. cars and aircraft).[3] By September 1938, *New Propeller,* the monthly newspaper of the unofficial aircraft industry shop stewards' organisation, already had a claimed circulation of 20,000 copies, with sales in 51 factories. In April 1940, the founding conference of the strongly CP-influenced Engineering and Allied Trades Shop Stewards National Council (E&ATSSNC) was attended by stewards from 107 factories, who agreed to expand *New Propeller* into a journal for the whole engineering industry.

Rather than take up the blunt (and ultimately counter-productive) instrument of imposing legislation making strikes illegal in the war industries – as in the First World War – Ernest Bevin, Minister of Labour in the newly-formed Churchill government, consulted the trade union leaders in May 1940 in order to gain their support for a 'no strike' policy.[4] The TUC accepted compulsory arbitration and respected the procedures set out in the *Conditions of Employment and National Arbitration Order* ('Order 1305') which made strike action unlawful (except in the most unlikely circumstances). In addition, the *Essential Works Order* (EWO) was passed early in 1941, restricting workers' right to leave their employment and reinforcing disciplinary procedures. However, in practice, this legislation significantly opened up opportunities for unions to intervene in war industry establishments. The EWO introduced a highly regulated system of workplace controls, but also – in the eyes of many workers – it abolished management's right to unilaterally determine working conditions and practices, and to arbitrarily 'hire and fire'.

Like the majority of the British people at this time, the trade union leaders placed the need for national unity, in the interests of the war effort, above all other considerations. To them, the conflict was 'a war against fascism' and/or 'a people's war' which required the unions' cooperation in order to maximise industrial production. The Communist Party had struck a discordant note when, in September 1939, it declared that the conflict with Germany was an 'imperialist' war in which the working-class should remain neutral.[5] This position was maintained – accompanied by support for strikes when they occurred – until June 1941, when the German army invaded the Soviet

Union. Thenceforth, the conflict was characterised by the Party as a 'war against fascism', in which support for the Allies was essential, and industrial output became paramount. At times the CP vied with the employers in the ferocity of their denunciation of workers taking industrial action.[6]

However, indications that all was not well amongst the lower orders continually bubbled to the surface during the war years. In March 1941, a *Mass Observation* report on morale amongst the Clydeside populace assessed the prevailing mood in stark terms:

> Clydeside workers are also having a war of their own ... they cannot forget the numerous battles of the last thirty years, and cannot overcome the bitter memory of industrial insecurity in the past ten years and their distrust of the motives of managers and employers ... (there is) a scepticism among many of the workers which is more deep and more bitter than anything we have found anywhere else ... [7]

In August 1942, the government's Chief Conciliation Officer in Scotland expressed concern to his Whitehall superiors about the growing influence in the engineering industry of 'old school' trade unionists, who still held the attitude that the unions' role was to combat the employer.[8] These workers, he reported, resented wartime union/management collaboration and actively opposed the formation of factory Joint Production Committees 'because they would enable the employers to intensify exploitation when peace returned'.[9]

In Clydeside factories like Albion Motors, this general legacy of the recent past was compounded and reinforced by a particular and identifiable continuity with proud traditions of working-class struggle. During the First World War, the factory shop stewards' convenor, Willie Gallacher, had also been chairman of the Clyde Workers Committee and played a leading role in the events on Clydeside at that time. In the 1939–45 conflict, Gallacher was Communist MP for West Fife and – as we shall see – maintained contact with the Albion Shop Stewards. The man who was convenor for most of the Second World War, John Gray, had commenced his apprenticeship in the Albion in 1917 and thus, by 1939, was still only 38 years old.[10] Gray was an active member of the Labour Party[11] and not a revolutionary, but his attitude to wartime issues seems to fall into what Croucher calls 'the ASE mentality'.[12] In other words, as a skilled engineer raised and rooted in a strong trade union environment, Gray's instincts would be to resist encroachments on his craft and working conditions no matter where they came from. Like their convenor, many Albion workers must also have spanned the 21-year gap between the two world wars in continuous employment with the firm, and so carried with them not only memories of recent injustices, but also direct experience of the Workers Committee period. In the way of shopfloor custom, apprentices and other new employees would soon be made aware of the factory's history, traditions and 'characters'.

❏ The Albion works

The Albion works is situated on the north bank of the Clyde, at Scotstoun, five miles west of Glasgow city centre. Albion Motors Ltd was established in 1899 and started building cars at its new Scotstoun works in 1903.[13] By 1906, 233 people were employed by the company. Just before the First World War, the company ended production of private cars and started to build commercial vehicles. This was influenced by the potential market in Commonwealth countries. This decision proved crucial in allowing the company to survive in a period when other car firms were going out of existence, and the workforce totalled 940 when the war started. By 1935, Albion was the sole survivor of the indigenous Scottish motor manufacturers.

During the Second World War, the factory built 7308 medium and heavy road vehicles for the War Department, including heavy artillery tractors. Handguns were also produced and, from 1942, a 'shadow' factory extension manufactured torpedo engines. The majority of the 2–3000-strong workforce were time-served skilled workers, but 'dilutees' – mainly women – were introduced from 1940 onwards. The company was a member of the Engineering Employers Federation.

The Albion shop stewards' records allow considerable insight into events and issues as they affected the Albion workers and their workplace organisation during the war years.[14] We will now discuss, in turn, union organisation in the factory, 'war' issues, disputes and strikes, the Joint Production Committee, and 'outside' issues. The information contained in these minutes and correspondence can help historians in assessing how workplace conflict and antagonisms were affected by the pressure of incessant and multi-sourced wartime calls for national unity, and by the accompanying demands of the war economy.

❏ Trade union organisation in the factory

Albion manual workers were 100 per cent union-organised. There were between 30 and 40 shop stewards in total who overwhelmingly represented AEU members (mainly skilled engineers), but the ETU (electricians), NUSMW (tinsmiths) and NSCSB (coppersmiths) also had shop stewards. In March 1941, female manual members of the TGWU were admitted to the Joint Shop Stewards Committee[15] and, from March 1942, representatives of the AESD (draughtsmen) and CAWU (clerical staff) participated on a 'watching brief' (i.e. they did not take part in any votes).[16] Shop stewards from the various unions met jointly on a statutory quarterly basis. At their Annual General Meeting each January, the stewards elected a convenor – for most of the war this position was held by John Gray of the AEU. A sub-convenor, a secretary and a treasurer (also AEU stewards), as well as the members of various sub-committees. The office bearers, plus five elected stewards, formed a Works Committee which conducted negotiations on factorywide issues, and were also members of a 16-strong Executive which met monthly. Both of these bodies included stewards from unions other than the AEU.[17]

Although, as indicated above, statutory meetings of the committees were specified, in practice many special meetings were called over a variety of issues. Stewards' meetings usually took place in the works canteen at the start of the day-shift (8 a.m.) to enable those on night-shift to attend. The stewards also organised mass meetings of the entire manual workforce on a regular basis to report back on negotiations, to seek endorsement of what they had done, and/or to urge support for a particular course of action. Union members could be (and were) disciplined for non-attendance at mass meetings.[18] A levy of 1d per month was collected from every union member in the factory and paid into a fund to meet expenses incurred by the stewards (e.g. for stationery and correspondence, delegation travel and subsistence, loss of earnings, etc). The stewards also raised money from the proceeds of a 'prize draw' they organised every Christmas.

Throughout the war, the Albion shop stewards jealously guarded trade union organisation in the factory, and were quick to respond to any perceived threat to union strength – from whatever quarter it came – as the following examples illustrate:

Non trade-unionists

One hundred per cent trade-unionism had been established amongst Albion manual workers before the war began. In addition, although the national union leaders had agreed that strikes would be illegal 'for the duration', Order 1305 and the EWO bestowed a degree of organisational legitimacy on unions which made it more difficult for employers to remove, ignore or bypass them. Nevertheless, in a period when the engineering workforce was both expanding rapidly and undergoing massive compositional changes, it was apparent that extreme vigilance would be necessary on the part of the shop stewards if they were to succeed in maintaining the closed shop. In June 1942, for example, two-thirds of the Albion workforce had commenced employment in the factory only in the previous two years.[19]

Thus, throughout 1940, the Albion shop stewards' Executive considered a number of cases in which new employees' apprenticeship lines had not been produced for inspection – or about which there was some suspicion. In two cases, inquiries to the new employees' union at their previous place of employment cleared up the matter.[20] However, in another instance, a man's lines were found to be forged and he was removed from the factory.[21] Two union members were also discovered to be heavily in arrears with their subscriptions and, the Executive informed the defaulters, unless this deficit was cleared within three weeks, a mass meeting would be called to request management to remove them from the factory.[22]

At the quarterly stewards meeting in December 1940, it was claimed that there was 'a great deal of negligence regarding the inspection of pence cards'.[23] The meeting agreed to carry out special inspections in two departments and to report all members over eight weeks in arrears to the convenor. Further to this, in August 1941, the stewards decided that during the imminent 'show of cards', every member's name, union branch, and state of subscriptions should be recorded and passed to the convenor. At the subsequent card inspection, a few members with heavy arrears were warned to clear them quickly, whilst it was discovered that a non-union member had been working in the factory for five weeks (he had subsequently been transferred to another job).[24] A few weeks later, an 'excluded member' (i.e. someone who had been expelled from the union) was uncovered and the stewards agreed to take steps to enforce his removal from the factory.[25]

KEEPING THE HOME FIRES BURNING

A more serious situation developed in the summer of 1942, when shop stewards were called to a special meeting to be told by the convenor that two 'anti-trade unionists' were causing a great deal of unrest in their departments due to their refusal to join the AEU.[26] These individuals, the convenor stated, had ignored his advice to apply for their release from the Albion and 'so prevent possible trouble'. Furthermore, the company was refusing to meet him to discuss the matter. The stewards agreed unanimously to call a mass meeting for the following morning, and to recommend giving two days notice of a complete withdrawal of labour if the two non-unionists were not removed from the factory. At the mass meeting, an amendment to the stewards' proposal was moved, seeking to reduce the strike notice to two hours, but this was 'defeated by a majority' in favour of the shop stewards' recommendation.[27] The following day, the convenor informed the stewards that arrangements had now been made for 'the release of the two men concerned', thus averting a strike.

Shortly after this event, it was recorded that another 'anti-trade unionist' had been 'persuaded to apply for his release'.[28] In May 1944, a mass meeting agreed to strike if two employees persisted in their refusal to join the union.[29] This incident was perceived to be 'an attempt to break open what has been a closed shop for years' but, after the intervention of the Regional Industrial Controller, the dispute was settled to the stewards' satisfaction.[30] However, within weeks, the issue of the removal of an employee with suspect apprenticeship lines was one of the sparks which triggered off the all-out strike in August 1944 (see below).

'D' factory

In August 1941, the convenor reported to the stewards on a meeting with the company about the new torpedo engine department which had just started production.[31] Such 'shadow' factories for war production were built by the government and run by the appropriate private firm under contract. Albion management's position was that this particular venture was a new factory operating under the control of the naval authorities and, therefore, totally divorced from the existing establishment. The convenor argued that the new facility was simply a part of the Albion works which had been set aside for the manufacture of torpedo engines – and he referred to it as the 'torpedo engine department'. Therefore, Gray stated, as factory convenor he had a right to discuss matters relating to this department, a claim refuted by management.

The issue was pursued by the stewards through the national engineering procedure agreement (the 'York memorandum') arriving at its final stage, a Central Conference, in January 1942, at which there was still 'failure to agree'. After hearing a report of this conference, the stewards agreed to ask for the support of the AEU Glasgow District Committee in seeking permission from the National Executive Council to ballot the Albion members for strike action.[32] They regarded the company's attitude as a restriction on the ability of the convenor to exercise his proper functions in relation to an area of the factory, and the District Committee gave their support to the stewards' request. Early in February, the AEU Executive rejected the Albion application on the grounds that 'no useful purpose would be served in taking a ballot vote upon a subject which the law forbids permission to operate' [33] (a reference to Order 1305 which decreed that disputes had to be resolved through arbitration).

However, the matter did not rest there, as by this time there already had been three AEU and two TGWU shop stewards appointed in the area under dispute, with the AEU shop stewards treating Gray as their convenor. By March 1942, shop stewards, from what was now referred to as 'D' factory, were participating along with the rest of the Albion stewards in factorywide meetings.[34]

Women

By the autumn of 1940, women had begun to appear in manual occupations as the Albion factory was geared to maximising wartime output.[35] Initially, the women were introduced into the stores area (21 females were employed there by the end of the year), and then into the casehardening (metal heat treatment) department. It was reported to the stewards' quarterly meeting, in January 1941, that management claimed the right, under the national agreement with the unions on 'dilution', to introduce female labour without consulting the 'men's representatives'. However, shortly afterwards, the company did discuss the introduction of women into the fitting shop with the convenor and the departmental stewards.[36]

In terms of trade union representation for the new women workers, as early as October 1940, the stewards' minutes record that: 'Brother Gray reported that he had been approached by the Lady Organiser of the Transport and General Workers Union regarding organizing women in the factory'. The reason for the intervention of the TGWU was that the exclusively craft unions in the engineering industry were also exclusively male, whilst the main union in the factory, the AEU – although it had been admitting noncraftsmen since 1927 – still debarred women from membership.

However, these policies did not necessarily imply that male workers were indifferent or hostile to the organisation of women in trade unions during the war. For one thing, if – as was clearly the case – females were going to be increasingly employed in what had traditionally been 'men's work' in order to maximise industrial output, then many men could see that it was also in their interests that the women's wages and conditions were not permitted to get too far out of line with their own. Otherwise, the attractions of cheap female labour to employers could become a threat to existing male conditions, and also encourage the expansion of women into other areas. Therefore, even the undoubted majority of male workers who did not support female rights to equal treatment could be made to see the desirability of women being unionised (although not necessarily by their union) and integrated into the workplace union organisation. (the disputes over women's conditions in the factory are discussed below).

Thus, in March 1941 – only a matter of six months after the introduction of women onto the Albion shopfloor we find the convenor welcoming two women shop stewards to their first joint stewards' meeting. One of these women, Mrs Robinson,[37] informed the quarterly meeting in December 1941 that a meeting of women workers had been held, and eight TGWU stewards and eight collectors (of union subscriptions) appointed. Mrs Robinson was also elected to the Executive Committee at the shop stewards' 1942 AGM and, at that meeting, she moved (seconded by Miss Greenan) that the committee recommend the admittance of women to the factory workforce's Mutual Aid scheme (for deaths, accidents, serious illness etc). This proposal was defeated by 24 votes to 9, in favour of an amendment stating that it was open to any committee member to propose alterations to Mutual Aid rules.

However, a few weeks later, the stewards were informed that the women's organisation in the factory was in 'a very poor state'.[38] Against a background of the massive recruitment of women engineering workers nationally by the TGWU, NUGMW and (latterly) the ETU, the AEU eventually decided to ballot its members on admitting women into the union.[39] The question was discussed at the quarterly stewards' meeting in the Albion in June 1942, when it was unanimously agreed 'that this committee do all in its power to make the Ballot vote re the admission of women into the AEU a success'.[40] Subsequently, Albion women workers were recruited by the AEU and a 'Sister Mackie' was elected as the women's provisional delegate to the District Committee.[41]

Apprentices

Engineering companies traditionally took the view that apprentices were 'bound' by their indentures to their employer for the duration of their training and that they therefore had no part to play in trade union matters. The lads themselves often saw the situation in a rather different light and, in the immediate prewar years, there had been considerable unrest over wages and conditions both nationally and in the Albion (the apprentices' disputes are discussed below.) Following widespread strike action in 1937, the AEU had been granted *de facto* rights to represent young workers and apprentices in national level negotiations.[42]

These developments had been an important factor in the AEU's decision to establish Junior Workers' Committees and, in June 1940, the Albion stewards agreed to notify apprentices of a Glasgow District Committee weekend school and to hand nominations to the convenor. Following further conflict over apprentices' bonuses, the convenor reported to the stewards that 'there had been some difficulty about the firm's attitude to the shop committee's intervention in apprentices' business'.[43]

What the apprentices thought about this intervention was reflected in a letter to the convenor from the 'Albion Apprentices Committee' in October 1941, in which they applied for representation on the shop stewards committee. It was agreed to approach management regarding the apprentices' application, but the company maintained their traditional stance and refused to allow the shop stewards committee to represent the lads.[44]

❑ 'War' issues

The stewards were involved in negotiations and activities around a number of issues which were uniquely related to the war itself. The factory organisation's approach to these matters reflected their

KEEPING THE HOME FIRES BURNING 37

commitment to trying to further their members' interests in many aspects of their lives and not just directly work-related issues.

The Blitz Fund

In March 1941, Clydeside experienced its heaviest German air-raid of the entire war. It was targgeted on John Brown's shipyard and the giant Singer factory in Clydebank located only two miles from the Albion works. A number of Albion employees suffered minor injuries while working in the factory – the most seriously injured were off work for only one week but the homes of many others were badly damaged.[45]

The stewards' quarterly meeting on 28 March discussed the situation and elected a sub-committee to investigate how best to help workers affected by the air-raids. This included forty married men completely bombed out of their homes. The sub-committee recommended the establishment of a relief fund to which all employees would pay 2d, 4d or 6d per week graded according to their wages.[46] The management agreed to match the workforce's contributions, and also to provide loans of up to £300 for pressing cases. The fund was to be administered by a committee consisting of eight manual and two staff workers, one shop steward and one management representative, with the secretary and treasurer appointed from the office employees. The stated aims of the 'Albion Air Raid Association' – usually referred to as the 'Blitz' Fund – were to assist employees affected by enemy action by means of:

1. Money grants, loans and material assistance in cases of hardship and distress;
2. A neighbourly interest in and personal visits to employees injured or otherwise rendered incapable of work;
3. Encouragement of those able to do so to return to work in order to further the war effort and their own rehabilitation.[47]

After the stewards met management and reached agreement on the proposals, they presented them to mass meetings of day and night shifts on 27 May, and these meetings gave their approval to the establishment of the fund.

However, on 1 August, a shop stewards' meeting agreed that unless management 'complete their arrangements' regarding their contribution, then the stewards would take over the administration of the fund. Management duly assured the convenor that they would get down to this as soon as possible. The quarterly stewards' meeting in October 1941 was informed that applications for payment from the fund were still being dealt with.

Fire guard and air-raid precautions

On 4 August 1939, a month before war with Germany was declared, the Albion shop stewards executive committee agreed to ask management to provide a scheme 'to safeguard workers' during air-raids. At the quarterly stewards' meeting in March 1940, a sub-committee was appointed to investigate ventilation problems throughout the works caused by the blackout precautions, and it was agreed to approach management about the situation. It was subsequently reported to the following quarterly meeting that the delay in improving ventilation was due to the Ministry of Supply refusing to issue a permit for the necessary materials.[48]

In July 1940, the convenor informed the stewards' executive that he had spoken to the Works Manager (William Pate) about the lack of proper warning when enemy air-raids were in progress, and had been told that warnings were in the hands of Scottish Fighter Command. The stewards reported the matter to the AEU District Committee for their consideration. However, it was later to emerge that the 'industrial warning' system as it affected the Albion works required the Observer Corps to report to the area headquarters, which was Yarrow's shipyard, whenever enemy aircraft were spotted within 15 miles of Glasgow.[49] Yarrow's then had to make contact with all other factories in the area and, it was claimed 'this would give an average of four minutes in which to take shelter'.

The situation during this period was that the government was seeking to establish a system of 'industrial Spotters' in order to minimise the disruption to production caused by factory evacuations when the public sirens sounded.[50] The government wanted workers to ignore the public sirens, continue working, and not seek shelter until the 'industrial warning' was given. Not surprisingly, these arrangements were viewed with apprehension and with no great enthusiasm by many workers. After discussing the matter with management, the Albion shop stewards accepted the 'industrial warning' arrangements to cover the day-shift, but agreed to seek further talks with regard to the night-shift.[51]

Between January 1941 and May 1944, the shop stewards were also regularly engaged in negotiating the conditions under which their members participated in fire-watching and air-raid precautions (ARP). Proposed changes in these conditions were reported to mass meetings of workers for their acceptance or rejection.

The initial fire-watching scheme was 'voluntary' but with the extremely persuasive Catch-22 proviso that those workers not registered as Albion fire-watchers could be liable to serve under the local authorities' compulsory scheme.[52] As the Albion PAD ('Passive Air Defence') Officer explained in a circular to employees:

> Such men are liable to perform duties up to a total of 48 hours per month, and their liability is not confined to the vicinity of their own homes but might imply duty at a factory anywhere in the local authority's area for longer hours than would be necessary at the Albion works.[53]

Following this communication, the Albion management made it clear that they proposed to tighten control over the operation of their own fire-watching arrangements (especially at weekends).[54] A special meeting of the shop stewards, in August 1941, had unanimously carried a motion rejecting such schemes 'unless trade union conditions apply'. However, after the passing of the Fire Prevention (Business Premises) Order in September 1941, a revised scheme was introduced. Under these regulations, all Albion male employees between the ages of 18 and 60 were legally obliged to participate in a round-the-clock fire-watching operation.[55] Over seven-day periods, workers were required to be at the factory for twelve-hour shifts which, whenever possible, were to be synchronised with their normal working hours. Any duties performed outside normal working hours would be paid at a subsistence rate of three shillings for twelve hours (or part thereof) plus travelling expenses. A rota would operate and no worker would be expected to perform ARP duties in more than one week in four. Management was responsible for the provision of sleeping accommodation, and for washing, sanitary and recreational facilities. A total of 1775 male Albion employees were registered under the scheme – including office workers whose union representatives had taken part in the negotiations with management.[56]

The Albion stewards endeavoured successfully to improve upon the conditions laid down in the legislation. Management agreed to consult the convenor on a weekly basis 'in order to ensure that proper and sufficient notice will be given to men called upon to perform a duty period under the compulsory scheme'.[57] Conditions related to the fire-watching scheme which were negotiated by the stewards included: the right of workers required to fire-watch during holiday periods to choose when to take their holiday entitlement; a stipulation that the day before and the day after a week's duty be taken as 'rest days'; substitutes to be permitted to enable workers to have one shift off during their duty week (or in the event of an emergency); and management to provide 'suitable social amenities'.

In fact, disagreement over the arrangements for the Easter holiday in 1942 led to a mass meeting which 'overwhelmingly' supported the stewards' recommendation to withdraw from the fire-watching scheme as it then operated.[58] Following management's acceptance that 'holiday periods (were) to be treated as special occasions and the rota shall not apply during such periods', a revised scheme was endorsed by a mass meeting on 13 May. Shortly after this decision, the unwillingness of management to accept 'rest days' falling on a normal working day (i.e. not on a Saturday or Sunday) was taken into the disputes procedure by the stewards.[59] Eventually, a mass meeting agreed to wait and see how things operated in practice.[60] Amendments to the fire-watching scheme continued to be the subject of negotiations between unions and management up to May 1944.

The Service Fund

Shortly after the outbreak of war, the stewards decided to test feeling in the factory regarding the establishment of a fund to help Albion employees who were serving in the armed forces.[61] Servicemen were required to support themselves and, in many cases, they also had to meet domestic commitments out of service pay. After receiving their members' support for this proposal, a five-strong committee operating under the control of the shop stewards was elected to take charge of the Service Fund.[62]

By February 1940, 850 workers in the factory had 'contracted in' to contribute to the fund.[63] Each serviceman began to receive payments of seven shillings per fortnight, and soon they were also being sent magazines and cigarettes by the factory organisation. Periodically, appeals were made by the stewards for more contributors to the fund, as well as for reading material. In 1943, the fund was still paying out about £70 per month to Albion employees in the services.[64]

One unfortunate incident in relation to this fund concerned a soldier, based at Aldershot, who wrote claiming he had not received any money or cigarettes for two months.[65] The shop stewards were concerned about the implications of this suggestion – the only complaint they ever received about the operation of the fund – and were particularly annoyed at the serviceman's threat to write to the Albion directors about the matter. He was informed that the directors had nothing whatsoever to do with the fund, and that a receipt with what clearly appeared to be his signature for payments covering the period in dispute had been received and was available for examination.[66] The stewards unanimously reaffirmed their support for those charged with administering the Service Fund.[67]

❑ Disputes and strikes

Despite the legal restrictions on strikes imposed under Order 1305, no fewer than 1785 strikes took place in 1943, whilst 2194, the total number of stoppages recorded in 1944, was the highest ever annual figure.

Engineering came second to coalmining as the most strike-prone industry but, in contrast to the mass action of the First World War, strikes in the industry were overwhelmingly confined to individual establishments and, in 1943–44, 90 per cent of them lasted less than one week.[68] Other forms of industrial action (e.g. overtime bans, work-to-rule) were not recorded in the official figures but, if events in the Albion are in any way typical, then these tactics must also have been widely employed. We shall consider, in turn: ongoing issues of contention in the factory; the strikes that occurred; and the attitude of the Albion shop stewards to disputes in other firms.

Ongoing issues
(i) Hours of work
The question of the length of the working week during wartime was an issue that engaged the shop stewards' organisation for the entire period of the hostilities. Widespread acceptance amongst workers of the need to help the war effort was offset by the physical, psychological and social effects of working and living under wartime conditions. Long shifts and few holidays, inadequate transport facilities, the debilitating impact of continuing air-raids and the blackout, combined with (in many cases) both marriage partners working long and perhaps different hours, meant that life was far from easy for working people. In October 1939, the second month of the war, the AEU District Committee informed members that the maximum

overtime permitted was 30 hours per month, rising to 45 hours in January 1940.[69] In June 1940, the Albion shop stewards asked management to accept that Saturday should not be regarded as a 'systematic overtime' day.[70] Management had offered an alternative day off 'where possible' to those required to work weekends, and mentioned the possibility of arranging 'rest weekends'.

In August 1940, the firm proposed a twelve-hour, six-day working week for all employees, stating that it was imperative to operate this as soon as possible.[71] The stewards argued that Saturday afternoon should be left free under any scheme, Saturday nightshift should not start until midnight, and stated that there would be no extra overtime while this work pattern was in operation. Assurances were also sought from management (and given) that consideration would be shown to workers wishing to attend trade union meetings. Although the company scheme was eventually put into operation, shopfloor discontent over it lingered and, before long, the stewards were discussing alternative proposals.

After lengthy discussion, the quarterly meeting in October 1941 decided by 19 votes to 15 to recommend acceptance of a three-shift system in preference to the existing scheme. Under these proposals, the only break in production would be from noon until 11 p.m. on Saturday which, with one half-hour meal-break per eight-hour shift, would give 147 and a half hours actual working time each week. Over a three week cycle, employees would work just over 49 hours per week on average and be paid for 64 and a half hours allowing for shift premiums to be paid. An amendment to put the matter before the workforce without recommendation was defeated by 22 votes to 13.

Management agreed to consider the new system provided that they could be assured it was acceptable to the workforce, but the three-shift proposals ran into further problems. Firstly, management raised the stewards' ire by appearing to turn a blind eye to what were described as 'two undesirable union members', whose presence in the factory led to the stewards giving 21 days notice of strike action unless the matter was resolved.[72] It was subsequently reported that 'the two defaulters with arrears in their union payments had been dealt with by Ministry of Supply authorities'.

A more serious problem arose over the Ministry of Labour and National Service's rejection of the three-shift system in February 1942.[73] The shop stewards believed that this rejection was due to a misunderstanding, and they agreed to approach local MPs immediately with a request that they speak to the Minister, Ernest Bevin, to get the proposal accepted. As a result of this strategy, Willie Gallacher MP informed the stewards that he had spoken to Bevin's second-in-command, George Tomlinson, and suggested that he communicate at once with his representative in the area, and direct him to meet the Albion shop stewards and management in order to get a satisfactory settlement'.[74] Tomlinson reconsidered the proposals, sanctioned the scheme, and forwarded an Emergency Order to the Albion management.[75]

The Ministry's decision to sanction the three-shift proposals had been preceded by a debate which encapsulated some of the issues which the shop stewards had to consider when formulating policy in wartime.[76] Those opposed to the three-shift system argued that it was not feasible, as shortages of skilled labour had already appeared in trying to meet output targets under the existing two-shift system. A 49-hour working week, they said, was not a reasonable effort during wartime. Furthermore, they claimed that the management's twelve-hour system actually allowed Albion workers more leisure time. In support of three shifts it was stated that there were sufficient numbers of the crucial skilled group, the machine setters, to run three shifts, and that past production hold-ups had been due to inefficient management. In terms of individual output, they argued that the number of hours worked was less important than the effort put in. The three-shift proposal gained the support of the stewards by a margin of 22 votes to ten.

In the summer of 1942, the stewards sought clarification from the Ministry of Labour and National Service regarding their attitude to workers refusing to work overtime. The Regional Officer replied that it was not policy '... to prosecute workers for failure to obey a direction regarding overtime unless the amount of overtime to be worked has been agreed between the Employer and the appropriate Trade union ...'.[77]

A few weeks later, the convenor reported that management were attempting to operate systematic overtime including Saturdays and Sundays.[78] In cases where an employee refused to work overtime, management intended to report 'offenders' to the National Service Officer so that 'directions' might be taken against them. The AEU District Committee had been in touch with the Engineering Employers' Association and the stewards agreed to apply for a Local Conference to get Albion management to accept 'that no worker shall be asked to work on Saturday afternoon except in the case of immediate emergency'.

Works Manager, William Pate, forcibly expressed his views on the matter of the length of the working week on several occasions. In March 1942, for example, when supporting management's twelve-hour shift proposals against the stewards' three-shift scheme, he quoted a Medical Research Council report which, he claimed, showed that 60 to 65 hours per week for men, and 50 to 60 hours for women, were not excessive 'under war conditions'.[79] In August 1944, when the factory was enmeshed in a web of interrelated disputes (see below), Mr Pate rejected the stewards' argument that Sundays – when double time was paid – had to be part of any systematic overtime pattern.[80] In a burst of patriotic fervour, the Works Manager reminded everyone of their obligation to do more 'in the National Interest'. He rejected complaints that the overtime hours permitted under compulsory regulations were too onerous for 'reasonably healthy people', and stated that failing to produce to everyone's greatest capacity was 'literally helping the enemy – and that aspect of the matter does not receive the consideration it should'.

(ii) Dilutees

Under the 1940 Extended Employment of Women Agreement, the engineering unions accepted that – strictly for the duration of the war – women could carry out tasks previously performed by male workers.[81] 'Dilution' was also permissible in upgrading male workers under the *Scheme for the Temporary Relaxation of Existing Custom,* thus we find Albion labourers being transferred to semi-skilled work, and semi-skilled machinists employed as skilled turners. Management and union had to agree to the upgrading at workplace level, and forward applications to joint management/union committees at district and national level for approval.

However, in the Albion – as elsewhere – the most contentious issue concerned the work to be carried out by female dilutees. After a few early hiccups over the question of the stewards' rights to consultation prior to the introduction of dilutees, the first problems over women arose in December 1940 (women had been employed in the factory for at least three months by then). The point at issue, and it was to prove a recurring one, was the company's alleged failure to pay agreed increases to women working in the Apprentice Training and Casehardening departments, and the stewards took the matter into procedure.[82] Early in 1941, it was noted that although 21 women had been started in the stores, no storemen had been upgraded.[83]

In March 1941, when the company proposed to introduce women into the fitting shop, protracted negotiations ensued over how these jobs were to be 'sub-divided' for the women to carry out, and how bonus earnings would be calculated.[84] In the course of these discussions, the stewards accused management of violating the national agreement by refusing to pay the full rate to women who had completed the agreed 32-week training period. This issue was settled by an agreement that for every grade of labour in the factory, women would receive one shilling per week below the male rate, the company claiming that this was justified to compensate for the women's lower efficiency.[85] In June 1943, these basic rates (nationally agreed rates plus national bonus) ranged from £3 14s 10d per week for female labourers to £4 14s 3d for female fitters and skilled machininsts.[86]

In March 1942, it was reported that workers in the fitting shop were no longer objecting to female dilutees, provided they were paid in relation to agreed job times.[87] Management agreed to issue details to every shop steward showing how the system would operate. In essence, 'simpler work' was to be performed by women under special supervision by a 'leading hand' who would be paid 1d per hour allowance to instruct and assist the women, and who would be responsible for all women's work in the section.[88] There would also be mixed male and female sections, whilst assurances were given that allotted job times would not be altered.

In June, the company told the convenor that they intended implementing their plans for the fitting shop without further consultation (i.e. women had still not been introduced into the area).[89] The convenor accused management of 'violating the constitution' and the stewards insisted on meeting the company to discuss the matter. An equally strong line was taken, in September 1942, when the shop stewards were informed that skilled setters had been asked to train women.[90] They unanimously agreed to instruct the setters 'that they are employed to set up machines for women to operate', not to train them.

Earlier in 1942, the question of women's work and its relationship to the factory bonus scheme had arrived at a Central Conference under the procedure agreement, before being referred back for local settlement.[91] There it was agreed that for the first eight weeks of a woman's probationary training, her time would not be 'charged' against jobs, 66 per cent of women's time would be charged between the 9th and 20th weeks, rising to 75 per cent between weeks 21 and 32. In 1943, the stewards tenaciously pursued alterations to the company's practice of paying the full rate to women when they were transferred to fitting work after 32-weeks training, but only paying whatever percentage they saw fit to women sent to welding or machining jobs. After eight months of negotiations, it was finally agreed that women sent to work in these areas would receive 85 per cent of the rate for up to eight weeks, and then be paid the full rate minus one shilling.[92] As late as June 1944 the right of shop stewards to insist on sanctioning any proposed extension of dilution was still being contested by management.[93]

(iii) Bonus
The most common cause of disputes in the engineering industry during the war was over bonus payments. In 1940, the wages of a skilled turner in the Albion were estimated to be £8 8s 6d for a 47-hour week.[94] However, while the nationally-agreed basic rate was only £3 7s 9d (40 per cent of the total wage), the factory premium bonus constituted around the same amount. Bonus payments were, therefore, extremely important to workers, and could be negotiated locally.

As well as ensuring that women were being accommodated within existing bonus systems (see last section), the factory stewards also had to deal with problems caused by the relatively high earnings attainable by pieceworkers in comparison to straight timeworkers. A national agreement guaranteed the earnings of the highly-skilled toolmakers, but no other non-production groups.[95] In December 1940, a shop stewards' meeting agreed to pursue a claim on behalf of the jig inspectors for inclusion in the toolroom agreement and, in February 1941, the Executive supported a similar claim from the gauge inspectors. At a Local Conference in August, the AEU Divisional Organiser – without consulting the other union representatives present – accepted management's offer to pay the inspectors the toolroom bonus, but only when the toolmakers' earnings rose above the inspectors'.[9]

Other groups in the factory whose case was taken up by the stewards' committee included the bar-auto section where, in October 1941, as a result of greater output, it was agreed that workers responsible for operating more than one machine should receive increased bonus compensation as tools and machines required more attention.[97]

The unreliability of the supply of materials in wartime also elevated the importance of guaranteed earnings for employees waiting for work through no fault of their own. At a Works Conference in August 1943, although the Works Manager did not accept the unions' claim that average bonus earnings should be paid to male fitters on waiting time, he agreed to look on the matter sympathetically provided any agreement was only for the duration of the war.[98] The convenor assured him that the unions had always accepted such arrangements and did not regard agreements in such circumstances as binding for all time.

On more general issues of principle related to bonus schemes, following swift union intervention early in the war, management had conceded that it was contrary to agreements for a ratefixer to take a job from one department to another in order to establish a time, and promised 'there would be no further attempt to do this'.[99] In April 1943, following union accusations that 'temporary times' for jobs had been unilaterally altered by management, the company spokesman complained of the longevity of some of these 'temporary' times, and of workers' continual refusal to permit changes in them.[100] (A detailed account of the factorywide strike over bonus earnings in 1944 is given below.)

The Albion management's decision to introduce an 'Employees Service Bonus' from 1943 onwards was regarded by the workforce as a removal of what they believed was their right to an 'Annual Bonus'.[101]

The company notice announcing the new scheme stated that, in the 1942 financial year, for every pound earned by employees with five years continuous service including overtime hours, but excluding war bonuses, and shift and overtime supplements, staff would receive 6d and timeworkers 3d, with the latter receiving a maximum payment of £3 7s 10d.[102] This would constitute the basic service bonus, but, in addition, employees who qualified would also receive 10 per cent of the basic payment for every year of service (up to a maximum of 20 years).

The manual workers' shop stewards argued that an 'Annual Bonus' had been paid since 1915 to all employees who had six months service, subject only to the company declaring a 7 per cent dividend to shareholders.[103] The new scheme, they stated, disqualified 70 per cent of the workforce who had less than the stipulated service, whilst it also represented a significant reduction in the amount of bonus to be paid to the minority who still qualified. The company's case was basically that payment of the bonus was a unilateral magnanimous gesture on their part, but that it had also been originally designed to attract and retain loyal workers. The stewards pursued a claim for retaining an annual bonus payable to all employees, but the matter was not covered by any local or national agreement. On the basis that the Albion management had worsened working conditions, the stewards utilised the procedures laid down under Order 1305 which bestowed power on the Minister of Labour to refer issues to arbitration.

The dispute was considered at a National Arbitration Tribunal in London, before a panel chaired by the Hon Mr Justice Simonds, on 1 March 1944.[104] The company emphasised that there had never been an agreement with the unions about the bonus, and all that had happened was that it had been decided to alter the conditions attached to payment, particularly, since two-thirds of the workforce had been sent to work in the factory by the Ministry of Labour. Mr A Maloney, the AEU National Executive member presenting the union case, expressed fears about other employers unilaterally worsening conditions in a situation in which workers were not free to leave and work elsewhere (under the EWO). Albion convenor John Gray pointed out that in 1915, when the company had introduced the bonus, shop stewards were not recognised for bargaining purposes, so the unions had been denied the possibility of discussing the question with management. Since that time, he claimed, it had not been a matter of contention as workers had become accustomed to receiving the bonus annually. From later documents (not to mention the general tenor of Mr Justice Simonds' contributions) it is clear that the NAT judgement went against the union.[105] One important side-effect of this dispute was the decision of the unions to withdraw from the factory's Joint Production Committee (see below). Another pointer to the existence of adversarial union–management relations was the anger of the workforce which was expressed at a mass meeting called to hear a report-back from the NAT. This was extremely strong in response to the company spokesman's seemingly derogatory remarks about the quality and motives of those workers recruited since the war had started.[106]

Strikes in the factory
To the recurring flames of discontent among apprentices over the length of their training period and the wages they received in return for the work performed, the war added more fuel. Male and female trainees

were coming into the engineering industry in considerable numbers and, after a relatively short training period, they could expect to earn more money than the apprentices.[107] The fact that the lads were often expected to help train the new higher-paid employees added insult to injury.

The 'Clyde Apprentices Committee' had been set up in March 1940 at a meeting attended by delegates from 35 major workplaces.[108] Following strikes in a number of firms early in 1941, by 15 March that year, an estimated 6000 Clydeside apprentices were on strike for a wage increase. On 12 March, the Albion convenor called the factory stewards to a special meeting to discuss the strike. He informed them that he had given management a list of all machines being operated by apprentices when they had walked out, and had told the company that these were now 'blacked'. Management, he said, had accepted this position 'rather than have trouble in the factory'. The stewards also agreed to a levy of one shilling per week from all male workers and 6d from females in support of the lads on strike. The apprentices returned to work on 17 March and a Court of Inquiry (set up by Bevin) established, for the first time, apprentices' wages at every age as a fixed proportion of the adult wage. Gray told the Albion stewards that he thought the results justified the apprentices' action.[109]

It was reported to the stewards' quarterly meeting in May 1941 that negotiations were continuing to try to resolve problems over 'inadequate job times and wrong classifications of machines' in the gear-cutting section. However, on 5 June the section went on strike and, the stewards were told, no attempt had been made by the company to involve the convenor.[110]

It was agreed that the gear-cutters had genuine grievances and that a financial appeal on their behalf should be made to the rest of the workforce. A special shop stewards' meeting on 13 June decided by 'an overwhelming majority' to recommend to the gear-cutters that they return to work to allow a Works Conference to take place on their grievances. It was also agreed that a representative of the strikers should be invited to attend the negotiations. The dispute was 'favourably settled for the strikers', and the gear-cutters expressed their appreciation for the shopfloor collections which had enabled payment of one full week's time rate plus £1 13s 0d to be made to every striker.[111]

In January 1942, a welder was suspended for three days for refusing to do more 'test pieces' than were normally required to satisfy periodic quality procedures.[112] An appeal was lodged against the suspension and the welders withdrew their labour for half a day in support of their colleague. On a number of other occasions – notably in cases involving non-unionists (see above) – mass meetings of the entire manual workforce voted to support the shop stewards' recommendations and give management notice of strike action but, in the event, a settlement was reached before the strike decision was implemented. However, the whole Albion workforce did withdraw their labour for eight weeks in the autumn of 1944. As indicated earlier, the strike was the culmination of a period in which discontent over a number of issues had been smouldering for some months.

Firstly, in May 1944, the stewards put forward proposals for changes in the premium bonus scheme, which they calculated would have increased earnings by around five shillings per week.[113] In addition, they wanted all timeworkers to be paid 100 per cent of the average pieceworker's bonus. In support of the claim it was argued that earnings were higher in other local factories, and that workers 'directed' to the Albion were greatly dissatisfied at having to work harder for less money. This was widely known and, as a result, men were reluctant to come and work in the Albion. Furthermore, it was stated, even with current job times some sections were finding it difficult to earn the existing 27.5 per cent national bonus. Management rejected the stewards' claim, stating that bonus times had not all been reviewed – as they should have been – prior to implementation of the 27.5 per cent national production bonus. The firm's spokesman also said that the national award of an eight-shilling differential on timeworkers' wages 'was expressly arranged to bridge the gap' with pieceworkers, and there would be no enhancement of either the bonus or timeworkers' rates. The company needed to compete after the war, and it was not possible 'to match the extravagant and short term policy of purely war-time concerns'.

The second issue in dispute at this time was overtime. At a meeting on 13 June 1944, management complained about the refusal of the maintenance workers to work at the weekend, and about the overtime ban in operation throughout the factory.[114] Overtime, they argued, could not be regarded as an integral part of the operations of the whole factory, but should be determined by requirements. For example, it was stated, maintenance and production needs should be separated, and there were also bottlenecks in some sections while others who had been busy were now searching for work. Arrangements had to be 'flexible' and, furthermore, 'Flexible overtime working should be coupled with flexibility of movement between job and job, men following the workloads and working where they were required'.

The stewards' case was a straightforward one. If there were to be regular overtime, then some of it should take place on Sundays when workers received double time on the basic rate. Overtime should not be confined to week nights when the premium was only time-and-a-third. Ex-convenor Gray presented much of the union case, pointing out that if – as had been stated – the company had cut Sunday overtime in response to Government appeals in the interest of national expenditure and to save fuel, then this should have been discussed with the unions. It was also the case, he claimed, that where bonus earnings in the factory were high they were coming under attack. With regard to management references to the desirability of flexibility, Gray argued that men gained knowledge of their jobs through experience and would be handicapped if asked to do unfamiliar work. The factory sub-convenor traced the origins of the discontent to the company's withdrawal of the 'annual bonus' which, he said, amounted to a reduction in wages. Now, workers were expected to suffer a further reduction due to the company's overtime plans. A further meeting of the two sides on 31 July failed to resolve the matter despite management invocations of 'the national interest', which apparently would be best served if the Albion employees worked overtime only in midweek.[115]

Although the rising level of discontent in the factory was widely acknowledged, management ignored the stewards' arguments, nor did the company representatives respond to a broad hint at the 31 July meeting, that if the question of bonus earnings could be disposed of 'the overtime question might decide itself'. A Works Conference took place in August, but failed to resolve the issues in contention. The final straw, as far as the unions were concerned, was when it was discovered that a new employee's apprenticeship lines were suspect.

A mass meeting was held on 29 August where, the shop stewards told the assembled workforce, they were defending conditions established during the war – not just on their own behalf but on behalf of the whole working class.[116] The AEU District Committee (DC) minutes record that the Albion workers decided 'to withdraw their labour until the man has been removed'.[117] However, this minute was amended at the following DC meeting to make it clear that the Albion convenor had informed the committee that 'a Bonus Question was also the subject of dispute'.[118] The individual with the suspect apprenticeship had been removed from the factory, but the workers decided to stay out over the bonus issue. On a roll-call vote, a minority on the DC opposed the strike and also voted against amending the minute. In fact, the strike was the first dispute officially supported by the District Committee since the war had started.[119] However, the union Executive then intervened to instruct the DC to call a meeting of the Albion membership in order that the Divisional Organiser (Robert Allan) might address them 'with the object of securing a resumption of work'.[120]

The Albion stewards delayed carrying out this instruction by convincing the DC that other unions with members on strike would also need to be represented. In the event, when the mass meeting eventually took place, Allan's endeavours on behalf of the Executive to secure a return to work still proved fruitless. The strikers gained the support of the AEU district shop stewards' quarterly meeting, who agreed that the DC should approach Glasgow Trades Council for financial support.[121] Delegations from the Albion travelled all over the country to raise money, and street collections were also organised as the strikers faced mounting financial hardship.[122] After eight weeks on strike, an AEU Executive instruction was supported reluctantly by the convenor. It was instructed that the members return to work, to allow negotiations to proceed, was carried at a mass meeting on 19 October.[123]

The workforce duly returned to work on 23 October.[124] The bonus claim was pursued through the procedure to a Central Conference, but the dispute was still not settled.[125] Meanwhile, the company had further muddied the waters by declaring a number of workers redundant, despite union opposition.[126]

At a meeting with the stewards in the factory on 21 November 1944, the company's statement recounted how the overtime ban in operation had, and continued to, affect bonus earnings, as waiting time and 'out of a job' problems gave rise to demands for average bonus to be paid.[127] Both sides, it was stated, had to show 'sufficient elasticity ... to avoid ordinary day-to-day questions becoming questions of so-called principle.' However, the Works Manager lamented: 'We are all aware that there is something like a state of guerilla warfare existing in some parts of the shop ... it goes under the name of non-co-operation ...'.

Negotiations dragged on into 1945, and the central issue of bonus payments still remained unresolved when the war ended.

Strikes in other factories

During the war years, a number of strikes took place in the engineering industry on Clydeside which were perceived to be of wider significance for the trade union movement. We discuss here disputes supported by the Albion shop stewards concerning, respectively, trade union organisation, the right to strike and equal pay for women.

The victimisation of the third AEU convenor in four months by management at British Auxiliaries in September 1940 was viewed by local union activists as a challenge which could not be avoided.[128] When the 250-strong workforce went on strike they received financial assistance from shopfloor collections, including the Albion, although the AEU Executive were pressurising the District Committee to end the dispute. The local engineering employers insisted on a return to work before any negotiations could take place, and were refusing to employ any British Auxiliaries worker. Meanwhile, the Ministry of Labour Conciliation Officer was reporting to his superiors that he judged the Albion to be one of the few factories which might deliver a threatened solidarity strike.

The Albion workers contributed £116 5s 9d to the strike fund but, on 26 October, in the seventh week of the dispute, convenor John Gray informed shop stewards of 'the gravity of the situation'.[129] Gray was part of a three-man AEU District Committee team who discussed the case with the Conciliation Officer trying to mediate between the union and the employers' association. In this capacity, Gray and the other delegates sharply disagreed with the union's spokesman who was widely perceived to be following Communist Party instructions not to antagonise the national union leaders and end the strike quickly. After two months, strikers started drifting back to work and the dispute ended without the victimised convenor being reinstated. Gray's role can safely be assumed to have had some bearing on later events (see below).

Although most of the participants were boilermakers, the AEU District Committee also became embroiled in a dispute at the North British Locomotive (NB Loco) works in December 1942. Some engineers had taken part in a sit-in strike over bonus payments, for which they were severely castigated by the District Committee, as well as being prosecuted and fined for contravening Order 1305. An Albion shopfloor collection of £53 18s 0d was sent to the strikers.[130] At a mass meeting of all Albion workers, the following uncompromising resolution was carried and sent to the Prime Minister with copies to the Minister of Labour and the Secretary for Scotland:

> This mass meeting of Albion workers view with grave concern the vicious sentence imposed on 91 workers employed in Queens Park Locomotive Works who had taken part in an illegal strike for the principle of upholding Trade Union Principles, and we demand the above mentioned sentence be remitted.[131]

Prior to the first AEU quarterly district stewards' meeting in 1943, a leaflet signed by a number of local stewards and condemning the Communist Party-led District Committee's role at NB Loco was distributed. Albion convenor Gray was amongst three District Committee members who signed the statement and were subsequently suspended from 'all offices under the jurisdiction of the District Committee for a period of one year' (by 13 votes to 11).[132] In a letter to the District Committee, the Albion shop stewards expressed the 'very serious view' they took at the penalty imposed on Gray, and requested the Committee to discuss the matter with a deputation of four stewards at their next meeting.[133] By 17 votes to 10 the DC agreed to hear the Albion deputation, who appealed to them to revise their decision in the interests of the unity of the Albion workers and because of the effect on the shop organisation.[134] A dozen union branches also expressed opposition to the DC's action in suspending the delegates.[135] At their next meeting, the District Committee resumed the discussion and, by a 12 to 8 margin, voted to rescind the suspensions 'providing the members will in future loyally abide by decisions passed by the DC and endorsed by the EC', with the minority wanting simply to rescind the decision with no strings attached.[136]

In November 1943, 16,000 of the 20,000 manual workers at Rolls-Royce Hillington plant, near Glasgow, downed tools in protest at a new grading system negotiated by the factory shop stewards on behalf of the 8000 females employed there. After almost two weeks of the strike, the Conciliation Officer and some of the stewards organised a ballot (with, at most, 30 per cent of the strikers taking part) which resulted in a return to work.

However, women at a number of other local factories had either joined the strike or voted to take action. Amongst these was the Barr & Stroud plant at Anniesland – about two miles from the Albion works – where 2000 women came out on strike on 13 December 1943, demanding a substantial wage increase. As at Rolls-Royce, the shop stewards committee was split, and the AEU Divisional Organiser insisted that a two-thirds majority was necessary for strike action. Initially, the male workers came out in support of the women, but they were persuaded by the union officials to return to work, although about one-third of the 1400 men came out again on 6 January 1944. The main AEU official involved at Barr & Stroud was Robert Allan who was in fact a former Albion shop steward and convenor. Allan had left the factory on being elected Divisional Organiser in 1941. As can be seen from the above account, Allan adopted an extreme 'constitutionalist' position during the dispute. The Albion shop stewards committee maintained their tradition of supporting those in struggle and raised a factory collection of £48 for the strikers. Although some improvements were made in the women's position, the strikers were unable to gain the support of the majority of male workers in the factory, or to spread the dispute to other establishments, and returned to work after four weeks.

❑ The Joint Production Committee

Criticism of the performance of British management was rife during the 1940–42 'production crisis'.[137] Widespread accusations of managerial incompetence and inefficiency were spiced with suspicions that some employers were sabotaging the war effort. In the engineering industry, pressures for worker participation in increasing production received a significant boost from the Communist Party's commitment to maximising output after the Soviet Union entered the war in June 1941. After some initial hesitation, the AEU took up the shop steward-initiated campaign for the establishment of, and union representation on, 'joint production committees' (JPCs) in every factory. Ernest Bevin, who regarded the JPCs as a step towards the attainment of class harmony, then persuaded the TUC General Council to overcome their fears of a Communist plot and lend their weight to the demands. In March 1942, the engineering employers, despite forebodings that their 'right to manage' was under threat, were also pushed by Bevin into signing a national agreement with the unions to establish JPCs in all workplaces with more than 150 employees.

In the Albion, the debate on the shop stewards' committee early in 1942 over the proposed introduction of a three-shift system reflected this concern with increasing output and efficiency (see above). In November 1941, the stewards had also sent a memorandum to the

Minister of Supply, Lord Beaverbrook, detailing the alleged underemployment of certain machinery in the factory.[138] Thus, on 17 April, shortly after agreement was reached at national level, the Albion shop stewards and management met to discuss setting up a 'Joint Production Consultative and Advisory Committee' in the factory.[139] In order to reassure workers that the national agreement's stated commitment to obtaining 'maximum output' would not result in a reduction in agreed job times, it was agreed to issue a joint union–management notice to this effect. Management deferred taking a decision on the unions' request that JPC members should be paid average bonus earnings for attendance at meetings. The national agreement only stipulated payment of the basic rate plus national bonus. It was further agreed that a maximum of ten representatives from both sides would attend JPC meetings. These proposals were carried by 'an overwhelming majority' at a mass meeting on 13 May and, in the ballot that followed, every 'workers' representative' elected to the JPC was a shop steward.

At the first monthly meeting on 13 June, held in the staff dining room, the Managing Director intimated that he would chair JPC meetings (in accordance with the national agreement). The shop stewards nominated their committee secretary, Tom Barr, to the joint secretariat, who were charged with the responsibility of issuing minutes and arranging meeting times and agendas. John Gray reiterated fears that reductions in job times would appear to be the result of high bonus earnings, since, he stated, this would 'destroy confidence and make much more difficult the purpose of the Committee'. The committee agreed unanimously that 'so long as individual operations remain unchanged' bonus times would not be altered. Management's offer to give a presentation, describing the production and related materials flow within the factory, was accepted by the stewards, and this duly took place at the July meeting.

Over the period that the Albion JPC met, the issues raised by the shop stewards tended to fall into two categories. First, matters which they believed were directly limiting production.[140] These included items such as a shortage of gauges and other instruments in the toolroom; the poor condition of machinery (e.g. grinders) and equipment (lifting gear in the machine shop); the inadequacy of the notification system for stocks of parts which were running low; the suggested provision of jig location devices and cradles to aid assembly operations. The second type of item brought before the JPC by the workers' representatives concerned issues which they argued had an indirectly adverse effect on production.[141] For example, what were described as 'longstanding complaints' included one concerning the ventilation system in the Heat Treatment section, the fact that there was only one cold water tap in the Repair Shop where workers needed to wash their hands before moving to new clean tasks, also the removal of a drinking tap from the Blacksmiths' Shop and the opportunity provided by the installation of new equipment to improve unpleasant working conditions in the Wash Department. In general, management indicated that they would investigate the points raised by the workers' representatives, and it was agreed that individual stewards would have the right to consultation regarding management actions. However, at the third JPC meeting, the chairman felt moved to tell the committee that it was only valid to raise matters about which they could do something, and that other complaints should be raised through the existing channels.[142]

If the stewards seemed to make the running in the JPC's first few months, by the November 1942 meeting management appear to have decided to try to set the agenda. Under the heading of 'efficient use of the maximum number of production hours', the Works Manager produced a graph of power consumption in the factory. He stated that this showed that power did not peak until half to three-quarters of an hour after starting time, whilst it started to dip half an hour before stopping times. The shop stewards argued that this pattern could be explained by a number of factors including the fact that the first part machined every day had to be inspected, messages had to be passed on at the start of a shift and machines cleaned before the shift ended and also because workers tried not to be late in getting to the canteen because of the limited food available. The company representatives also raised the issue of getting people to work on Saturday afternoons. A particular problem was highlighted in the gear section, where the grinders were refusing to work then, even on urgent jobs. The union convenor suggested that workers were entitled to this 'minimum period of recreation' but, he ventured, the company might get a better response if they agreed that those working Saturday should get Sunday off (and vice versa).

At the following JPC meeting, the Works Manager stated that the company were prepared to investigate and, if possible, remedy any factor holding up production.[143] But, he argued, the basic problem was how to create a definite will to improvement among the mass of the workforce. This line was continued following the receipt of a letter from the Ministry of Supply's Director-General of Mechanical Equipment, placing an urgent order for Heavy Artillery Tractors and underlining the need for 'maximum effort' to meet delivery dates.[144] In order to comply with the government's needs, the JPC were told by the Works Manager, 'more production hours and harder work would be required from the factory personnel'. Convenor Gray offered the opinion that increased output was more likely to result from higher bonus earnings than from longer hours, while consideration should be given to introducing bonus schemes to sections which did not have them. However, it was agreed that the letter from the Ministry of Supply should be posted up around the factory, and that either the Works Manager or a Ministry representative could address a meeting of the whole workforce as the stewards had proposed.

At the same JPC meeting, Gray claimed that, despite management assurances and the agreement reached at the first JPC meeting concerning bonus times, there was evidence that long-established job times were being cut. These he detailed in a letter to management with examples from the Assembly Department, the bar-auto section and the gear-cutting section.[145] In the Fitting Shop, Gray listed one job originally timed at 25 hours, which had been reduced to 20 hours in July 1942, and then cut again to 15 hours in October; in November, another job time had been slashed from 40 to 28 hours. Works Manager Pate argued that although the convenor's claim was correct, these were temporary times which had been allowed to continue due to abnormal wartime conditions. At the JPC, Pate had emphasised the need to overcome 'the long standing Albion tradition of limiting bonus earnings' and, in March, he returned to this theme, stating: 'If workers' representatives could persuade the factory personnel to go all out, they will be overcoming the prime factor which kept down output and their own bonus.'[146] All other questions dealt with by the JPC, Pate argued, were insignificant in comparison with this issue. At the May 1943 meeting, although management offered an attendance payment of five shillings to workers attending JPC meetings, and the unions raised the question of office staff representation, this proved to be the last occasion the Albion committee met. The June meeting was postponed, and when the chairman ruled as incompetent business a union item – the service bonus scheme and its effect on production – due for discussion at the August meeting, the workers' side resigned from the JPC.[147] Their resignation letter

KEEPING THE HOME FIRES BURNING

referred to the 'untenable' position they found themselves in as a result of widespread dissatisfaction in the factory over the service bonus scheme.

As well as the factory JPC, the Albion workforce were also represented at meetings of Glasgow District Trade Unions Production Committee. This body operated under the umbrella of the TUC and often co-sponsored meetings and conferences with Glasgow Trades Council. They recommended factory JPCs set and publicise production targets, provide suggestion boxes in every shop, report back on a regular basis, investigate cases of scrapped jobs, arrange for non-manual participation in JPCs, and fully liaise with and submit minutes of factory meetings to the district organisation.[148] In April 1943, these recommendations were adopted at a conference attended by 119 delegates from engineering factories and shipyards (including the Albion), plus 137 other union representatives.[149] The main speaker, Garro Jones MP, Parliamentary Secretary to the Minister of Production, 'paid glowing tribute to Glasgow's contribution to the country's production effort', favourably mentioning the Scottish figure of 28 per cent of establishments with a functioning JPC. Those attending the conference were reminded: 'We have a say if we see anything wrong in the running of the factory or the shipyard ... the motive in the trade union movement ... is not to help the employers out of a Jam but to help the war effort ...'.

❏ 'Outside' issues

Early in the war, 'a high powered group' was given the task of getting the cooperation of the trade unions in Scotland and persuading them to 'come out openly against communist influence on the shop floor'.[150] The particular fear haunting the government was the re-emergence of a militant rank-and-file organisation similar to the Clyde Workers Committee, and the threat that such a body would pose to the war effort. The actions of the Scottish TUC and the AEU, the most important union in arms production, were regarded as early successes in this campaign to deter workers from associating with 'unofficial' bodies.[151]

When a circular from the aircraft shop stewards organisation (the ASSNC), inviting the appointment of delegates to a conference in Birmingham, was read out at the Albion executive meeting in March 1940, its competence as an agenda item was challenged by Robert

Allan.[152] However, the convenor ruled that the matter should be discussed at the forthcoming stewards' quarterly meeting, leading Allan to request that his dissent be recorded.[153] At that meeting, Allan moved against sending delegates to the ASSNC conference and won the vote 21 to 10.[154]

A letter from the (newly-established) E&ATSSNC 'Glasgow Provisional Committee' was considered at the April meeting of the Albion stewards executive. Discussion of the issue took place against a background of the receipt of an AEU Executive circular warning that any steward who attended unofficial conferences at which AEU business was discussed would lose their credentials.[155] Nevertheless, the proposal to send delegates from the Albion was carried by nine votes to two. At the following stewards meeting, a vote of censure on the executive for going against previous instructions was moved, again by Allan, but was defeated by 15 votes to 11.[156] However, in their report-back, the delegates who attended the Glasgow conference recommended that future meetings called by the organising body should not be supported, and this was endorsed by the stewards. In March 1941, when a request to send delegates to another unofficial conference was considered, it was agreed that stewards wishing to attend could do so, but not in their official capacity.[157]

In February 1943, the North British Locomotive shop stewards called a meeting to discuss the fines imposed on workers in the factory (see above).[158] Given the close involvement of their convenor in the NB Loco dispute and the resolution carried at the mass meeting on 11 February, it appears extremely likely that the Albion was one of the 17 factories represented at this meeting. This event was of some significance, in that it was followed shortly afterwards by the formation of a revived (and Trotskyist-initiated) Clyde Workers Committee, in which stewards from several of the factories represented at the NB Loco meeting played a leading role.[159]

In April 1944, following a wave of strikes in mining and engineering, Ernest Bevin introduced Regulation 1A.A which imposed penalties of five years' imprisonment or a fine of up to £500 on anyone instigating an unofficial strike.[160] This measure was accepted by the TUC and, the Ministry of Labour stated, the Regulation 'should strengthen the hands of the Trade Unions in dealing with irresponsible elements'. The Albion shop stewards passed a resolution condemning the TUC for endorsing the legislation.[161] The AEU District Committee unanimously carried a similar resolution, moved by John Gray, which protested:

> ... against the action of the TUC in endorsing the Regulation which allows for the imposing of a penalty of five years penal servitude on any of our fellow members who move for strike action in the workshop. We also protest against the action of our President in agreeing that this is a fit and proper Regulation. We believe that this Regulation gives a licence to the Employers of Labour to continue their policy of provocation.[162]

Earlier, in January 1941, the government had suppressed the Communist Party newspaper, the *Daily Worker,* under emergency powers Regulation 2D, on the grounds that it was 'formenting opposition' to the prosecution of the war.[163] Protest at this action increased in volume, especially after Russia's entry into the war, and was especially powerful in the engineering industry where the AEU gave its support to the campaign for the ban to be lifted.[164] On 13 December 1941, the Albion shop stewards decided 'by an overwhelming majority' to send three delegates to a conference in Glasgow in order 'to bring pressure to bear for the return of the *Daily Worker*'. (The ban on the newspaper was lifted in September 1942.) Further indication of the different light in which the Soviet Union was now viewed can be seen in the letter which the stewards received from the Glasgow District Labour Party in January 1942, asking the committee to organise a 'Flag Day Collection' in the factory for the Soviet Medical Aid Fund.[165] The request met with unanimous approval and it was decided to ask the management for authority to make arrangements for the collection which raised £82 1s 10d.[166]

A question which proved more contentious was an invitation to the stewards to send a delegation to a conference organised by the Glasgow & District Women's Parliament.[167] A proposal that the stewards use their influence with the women in the factory to appoint delegates only defeated the amendment, 'that no action be taken', by 15 votes to 11.

❑ Conclusions

'Thereafter there was complete cooperation between Government, employers and trade unions at every level of industrial decision.'[168]

Francis Williams' assessment, in his history of British trade unionism, of the effect of Ernest Bevin's appeal to the unions in May 1940 for total commitment to the war effort, represents a widely-held opinion about wartime industrial relations in Britain. Those who accept and/or promote this idealised picture have a major problem in then explaining how it could be that 6533 strikes were officially recorded in the four years, 1941–44, *after* Bevin's appeal.[169] We would suggest that the evidence from the records of the Albion Motors Shop Stewards hammers another nail into the coffin of that particular historical misconception.

The apparent contradiction in the day-to-day attitudes of many trade union activists – between the desire for social change and the responsibility simultaneously to operate as representative and negotiator within a restrictive economic structure – can be felt even more sharply during wartime. Pressures, from many quarters, to do everything possible to help the 'war effort' – especially when the war is portrayed as a struggle to the death against fascism – can lead to prostration before the demands of that unyielding taskmaster 'the national interest'.

How then can we summarise the Albion shop stewards' response to these pressures in terms of the issues that arose during the war?

Whilst it is clear that the stewards accepted wartime burdens such as excessive working hours, 'dilution' of skilled tasks, compulsory firewatching duties, etc., they always sought to preserve their right not just to consultation but also to retain the principle of negotiation. When it came to union organisation, the evident determination to ensure that every employee was a union member undoubtedly reflected a common view, reinforced by experience in the 1920s and 1930s, that non-unionism, whether in peacetime or war, operated only in the employer's interests. The demise of the JPC and the positions struck by the two sides at JPC meetings can be viewed as being due either to the parties having accidentally stumbled into conflict, or else as a result of a conscious strategy being pursued by either or both parties. But what is unmistakable is the impression that what is taking place at the JPC is the pursuit of bargaining objectives by other means, and in an atmosphere of adversarial relations.

Generally, the issue that recurred most often in terms of the cause of union–management conflict was the question of bonus levels. Considering that approximately 40 per cent of the weekly wage was accounted for by bonus payments negotiated at factory level, this is hardly surprising. Despite a number of bonus disputes which led to some form of industrial action, and despite periodic expressions of discontent from timeworkers, the only strike of any duration took place in 1944. The date is significant as war production was starting to be wound down, and both sides undoubtedly had at least one eye on staking out positions in preparation for the situation after the war. Management's knowledge of the actual state of the order-book always gives them a certain strategic advantage over their employees in such situations. In this instance, it would appear that awareness of falling demand for the factory's products perhaps explains why the company was prepared to sit out an eight-week stoppage.

But how was it that the Albion stewards were apparently able to consolidate their position within the factory and maintain an independent trade union standpoint despite the multitude of wartime pressures?

First, the general environment was in some ways favourable. The manpower needs of the armed forces combined with the demand for workers in the war economy to create shortages of labour from 1940 onward. A transformation of the situation that had prevailed for most of the interwar period. The fact that, under EWO regulations, workers could not be dismissed arbitrarily, also helped to regenerate confidence in trade union rights and activity. However, the Albion was also one of a small number of Clydeside engineering factories which were notable in that the stewards and workforce consistently supported workers involved in other strikes in the area, including some which received little or nothing in the way of encouragement from their unions or the general public. Thus, there were clearly factors at work which not only ensured that conditions within the Albion would be rigorously defended, but which also influenced the attitude of the stewards towards wider labour movement issues.

Many Albion workers embodied the twin traditions of pride in the skilled character of their jobs along with a strong commitment to trade unions which defended those crafts and improved working conditions. Furthermore, these deeply-rooted attitudes were reinforced by radical political traditions, with the two demonstrably fusing during the First World War in the Workers Committee movement. Although we have no detailed documentary evidence from the Albion records, we can safely say that it would be highly unusual if a large Clydeside engineering factory during the Second World War had no members of the Communist Party in its workforce. In the autumn of 1940 (i.e. prior to the CP's huge increase in membership later in the war) a donation to the *Daily Worker* Fighting Fund was made by supporters in the Albion.[170] From some of the issues raised at shop stewards meetings and the discussion that followed, it also seems clear that the CP did indeed have a presence in the factory. However, in comparison to the extreme 'productionist' stance taken by shop stewards' organisations in some other establishments,[171] developments in the Albion (e.g. over the JPC) suggest that the CP was not in a dominant position in the Albion shop stewards' organisation.

Events around the North British Locomotive prosecutions in 1943 and the subsequent suspension from office of the Albion convenor, John Gray, indicate contact (at the very least) with the Trotskyists of the Workers' International League (WIL). In the series of local engineering disputes in 1943 (NB Loco, Rolls-Royce, Barr & Stroud), stewards employed in these factories and with some kind of links to the Workers' International League, continually appear. Harry McShane, who was employed by the *Daily Worker* at the time, names the Albion as one of the plants where the Trotskyists got support.[172] However, given that almost 4000 strikes took place in 1943–44 against a background of opposition from the trade union leaders and the Communist Party, it is not surprising that those who were prepared to openly support strikers were 'cutting with the grain' amongst a not insignificant stratum of workers. It seems more likely that this was the basis of the relationship between the Trotskyists and the Albion shop stewards, rather than that the WIL were the 'guiding hand' behind the scenes.[173]

That there were political factors in play which underpinned the Albion stewards' approach to wartime issues therefore seems clear. The records tell us that this was not a group of workers concerned only with narrow 'economistic' issues. The fact that the stewards were split 15 votes to 11 on whether to support the 'Women's Parliament' conference, for example, shows that differing views were held on this question. Also, the involvement of the stewards in the Blitz Fund and the Service Fund was not some kind of charitable sideline activity, but a reflection of their perception that they had a responsibility towards the people they represented in the widest sense, both inside and outside the factory. Their ideology was robustly collectivist.

During the First World War, the shop stewards' movement was led by socialists who openly sought to encourage strikes for political objectives. In the Second World War, the organisation which many militants belonged to or looked to, the Communist Party, was implacably opposed to the development of such a strategy. Although there were twice as many strikes in 1941–44 as there were in 1915–18,[174] the disputes in the Second World War were overwhelmingly small and localised unlike the mass action of 1915–18. In the absence of a powerful shop stewards' *movement* in the Second World War which sought to unite and support striking workers, individual, or groups of, stewards who stood in the tradition of militant trade-unionism had to content themselves with engaging in and supporting struggles as and when they arose. Thus, even although there were many more strikes than in the First World War, much of the activity of individual factory organisations seemed 'ungeneralizable' and has remained hidden from the gaze of historians. Hopefully, this contribution which relies heavily on the Albion shop stewards' surviving records will help in the process of filling this massive gap in our historical knowledge.

NOTES

Abbreviations used

AEU: GDC	Amalgamated Engineering Union: Glasgow District Committee.
ASSC	Albion shop stewards committee.
ASSEC	Albion shop stewards executive committee.
JPC	Joint Production Consultation and Advisory Committee.
U–M	Union–management meeting in factory.
WC	Works Conference under national disputes procedure.
LC	Local conference under national disputes procedure.
NAT	National Arbitration Council, London, 1 March 1944

1. To underline the relative historical proximity of the two wars, a similar timespan from 1993–94 would take us back to the late 1970s – the period of the Industrial Relations Act, the UCS work-in, the release of the Pentonville dockers, Saltley Gate and the national miners' strikes.
2. All references to the Workers' Committee in this paragraph are drawn from James Hinton, *The First Shop Stewards Movement* (Allen and Unwin, 1973).
3. All references to the Communist Party and the shop stewards movement in this paragraph are from Richard Croucher, *Engineers At War 1939–1945* (Merlin,1982).
4. Ibid.; p. 89; Croucher argues 'Order 1305 had grown organically out of the close relationship that Bevin enjoyed with senior trade union officials'.

5. Angus Calder, *The People's War: Britain 1939–45* (Pimlico,1992) p. 59.
6. James Hinton, 'Coventry Communism ; A Study of Factory Politics in the Second World War', *History Workshop Journal*, no. 10, Autumn 1980, pp. 96–97.
7. Croucher (1982) *Engineers* pp. 118–119.
8. R. Croucher 'Communist Politics and Shop Stewards in Engineering 1935–46', unpublished PhD thesis, Warwick University, 1978, p. 341.
9. Ibid.; p. 340.
10. NAT minutes pp. 19–20.
11. Gray stood unsuccessfully as an AEU delegate to the 1942 Labour Party Conference; see Croucher (1978) p. 432.
12. Croucher (1982) *Engineers* pp. 168–173.
13. All information about Albion history from A Craig MacDonald and A S E Browning, *History of the Motor Industry in Scotland,* (paper presented at the meeting of the Institution of Mechanical Engineers in Glasgow,1961).
14. The hand-written minutes of the shop stewards' meetings only cover the period from August 1939 to October 1942. However, there are typed minutes of all Joint Production Committee meetings up to August 1943 (when the committee was disbanded), typed and hand-written minutes of union–management meetings, and copies of the stewards' correspondence, covering the entire period of the war. We also had access to the minutes of the AEU Glasgow District Committee. For the sake of appearance and brevity, where it is clearly stated within the text when a particular meeting took place we have not given a reference.
15. ASSC minutes 12 March 1941.
16. ASSC minutes 27 March 1942.
17. ASSC minutes 17 January 1942.
18. AEU:GDC minutes 7 April 1944. For remaining at work during a mass meeting, the Albion stewards reported a number of workers to the AEU District Committee. Those who apologised or appeared before the DC were fined 2s 6d, whilst absentees were fined 5 shillings.
19. NAT minutes p. 13
20. ASSEC minutes 30 March 1940; 31 May 1940.
21. ASSEC minutes 27 July 1940.
22. ASSEC minutes 26 October 1940.
23. Members paid their subscriptions at the union branch which – in the AEU and other unions involved – was geographically, not workplace, based. Therefore, shop stewards periodically inspected members' union cards to check that their subscriptions were up to date. However, the TGWU did collect at the workplace.

KEEPING THE HOME FIRES BURNING

24. ASSC minutes 26 August 1941.
25. ASSC minutes 17 January 1942.
26. ASSC minutes 5 August 1942.
27. ASSC minutes 6 August 1942; since the minutes often recorded mass meeting decisions being taken by an 'overwhelming majority', the formulation 'by a majority' suggests that there was significant support for the amendment.
28. ASSEC minutes 24 August 1942.
29. WC minutes 13 May 1944.
30. AEU:GDC minutes 5 May 1944.
31. ASSC minutes 1 August 1941.
32. ASSC minutes 17 January 1942.
33. AEU:GDC letter 13 February 1942.
34. ASSC minutes 27 March 1942.
35. ASSC minutes 20 September 1940. In the engineering and metal industries, the female wartime workforce peaked at more than 1.5 million. Calder *People's War*, p. 334.
36. ASSC minutes 28 March 1941.
37. Women are referred to as 'Mrs ...' or 'Miss ...' throughout the minutes.
38. ASSC minutes 18 February 1942.
39. Calder *People's War*, p. 349. Between 1939 and 1943, the AEU's national membership increased from 413,000 to 909,000, with 308,000 recruits in 1943 alone. In that year, the TGWU became the first union with over one million members.
40. ASSC minutes 26 June 1942. See also James B Jefferys *The Story of the Engineers* (AEU, 1946), p. 260. Following a 'decisive vote' in favour, women were admitted to the AEU from 1 January 1943, and 138,717 joined the union in the first year.
41. AEU:GDC minutes 29 November 1944; 24 December 1944.
42. Jefferys *Story of*, p. 245.
43. ASSC minutes 27 July 1940.
44. ASSC minutes 26 December 1941.
45. ASSC minutes 28 March 1941.
46. 'Blitz Committee' minutes (undated).
47. 'Albion Air Raid Association' notice (undated).
48. ASSC minutes 25 April 1940.
49. ASSC minutes 4 January 1941.
50. See Croucher (1982) *Engineers*, pp. 117–122 regarding attitudes to the 'industrial warning' system.
51. ASSC minutes 4 January 1941.

52. ASSC minutes 9 September 1941.
53. ASSC minutes Letter from I MacGillivary 28 August 1941 'Passive Air Defence' operated under the jurisdiction of the Ministry of Supply.
54. ASSC minutes 1 January 1942.
55. ASSC minutes 9 October 1941.
56. Document dated 9 October 1941.
57. ASSC minutes 17 January 1942.
58. ASSC minutes 3 April 1942.
59. ASSC minutes 25 June 1942.
60. ASSC minutes 25 June 1942.
61. ASSC minutes 22 December 1939.
62. ASSC minutes 6 January 1940.
63. ASSEC minutes February 1940.
64. Service Fund Balance Sheet 1943.
65. Letter to J Buchan 27 June 1942.
66. Ibid.
67. Ibid.
68. Calder *People's War*, p. 395.
69. ASSC minutes 28 October 1939; 6 January 1940.
70. ASSC minutes 27 June 1940.
71. ASSC minutes 4 September 1940.
72. ASSEC minutes 28 November 1941.
73. ASSC minutes 18 February 1942.
74. Letter from W Gallacher MP, 17 March 1942.
75. Letter from G Tomlinson MP, 13 March 1942.
76. ASSC minutes 11 March 1942.
77. ASSC minutes 26 June 1942.
78. ASSEC minutes 29 August 1942.
79. U–M minutes 8 March 1942.
80. WC minutes 2 August 1944.
81. Croucher (1982) *Engineers*, pp. 79–80.
82. ASSC minutes December 1940.
83. ASSC minutes 4 January 1941.
84. ASSEC minutes 28 March 1941.
85. ASSC minutes 25 October 1941.
86. Document dated June 1943.
87. ASSC minutes 27 March 1942.
88. Document dated 5 April 1942.
89. ASSC minutes 5 June 1942.
90. ASSC minutes 12 September 1942.

91. Document dated 6 March 1942.
92. Correspondence dated 27 March 1943; 9 April 1943; 30 September 1943 and 12 November 1943.
93. AEU:GDC minutes 16 June 1944.
94. Undated document.
95. Jefferys *Story of,* p. 260. The Toolroom Operatives Agreement of June 1940 guaranteed toolmakers the average earnings of skilled workers on piecework in the same firm (or district). Other skilled groups of time-workers (e.g. inspectors, maintenance) were not specifically covered by a national agreement until January 1942.
96. ASSC minutes 26 August 1941.
97. Document dated 4 October 1941.
98. WC minutes 5 August 1943.
99. ASSEC minutes 26 January 1940.
100. U–M minutes 2 April 1943.
101. Letters to Oliver Lyttleton MP, Minister of Production, and Ernest Bevin MP, Minister of Labour (25 August 1943).
102. Company notice (undated).
103. NAT minutes p. 3.
104. Ibid.
105. Ibid.; see also U–M minutes 13 June 1944.
106. Letter to company following mass meeting, March 1944.
107. Croucher (1982) *Engineers,* p. 124.
108. Ibid., p. 123. See also pp. 121–3 re national developments.
109. Croucher (1982) pp. 235–236 state that up to 7000 Clydeside apprentices were on strike in March 1944 over the 'Bevin Boys scheme'. It is not known if the Albion apprentices took part in this dispute.
110. ASSC minutes 11 August 1941.
111. ASSC minutes 1 August 1941.
112. ASSC minutes 17 January 1942.
113. U–M minutes 9 May 1944; WC minutes 26 May 1944.
114. U–M minutes 13 June 1944.
115. U–M minutes 31 July 1944.
116. Croucher (1978), p. 370.
117. AEU:GDC minutes 30 August 1944.
118. AEU:GDC minutes 13 September 1944.
119. Croucher (1978), p. 370.
120. AEU:GDC minutes 20 September 1944.
121. AEU:GDC minutes of quarterly meeting of shop stewards, 1 October 1944. AEU:GDC minutes 4 October 1944.

122. Croucher (1978), pp. 370–371.
123. AEU:GDC minutes 18 October 1944. Croucher (1978), p. 371, states that the return to work was carried by only one vote.
124. WC minutes 24 October 1944.
125. AEU:GDC minutes 13 December 1944; discussion of the bonus was taken up again in negotiations in the factory in 1945.
126. AEU:GDC minutes 1 November 1944.
127. U–M minutes 21 November 1944.
128. See Croucher (1982) *Engineers*; pp. 100–107 for background to British Auxiliaries strike (n.b. the 'J Grey' [sic] mentioned is undoubtedly John Gray); pp. 187–189 for North British Locomotive dispute; pp. 285–293 for Rolls-Royce and Barr & Stroud strikes.
129. ASSC minutes 26 October 1940.
130. Receipt dated 15 February 1943.
131. Copy of resolution sent to Prime Minister, Winston Churchill MP.
132. AEU:GDC minutes 11 August 1943.
133. Letter to AEU:GDC 15 August 1943.
134. AEU:GDC minutes 18 August 1943.
135. AEU:GDC Correspondence Sub-committee minutes 20 August 1943; 27 August 1943.
136. AEU:GDC minutes 25 August 1943; Croucher (1982) *Engineers*, pp. 187–189, comments upon the DC's decision to suspend Gray and the other two delegates, but seems unaware that this was rescinded two weeks later.
137. James Hinton 'The Citizen on the Shop Floor: The Idea of Democracy in the British Engineering Industry, 1939–48', Paper given at Glasgow University, 24 April 1992, for background information to JPCs.
138. Letter dated 28 November 1941.
139. JPC minutes 17 April 1942.
140. JPC minutes 30 July 1942; 15 October 1942.
141. JPC minutes 20 August 1942; 17 September 1942.
142. JPC minutes 20 August 1942.
143. JPC minutes 17 December 1942.
144. JPC minutes 25 February 1943.
145. Letter dated 14 March 1943.
146. JPC minutes 18 March 1942.
147. Letter dated 31 August 1943.
148. Glasgow Trades Council Circular and report of 3 April conference, 26 April 1943.
149. Ibid.

150. Ian McLaine, *Ministry of Morale; Home front Morale and the Ministry of Information in World War II* (Allen and Unwin, 1979) p. 192.
151. Ibid.
152. Allan later became AEU Divisional Organiser – see above.
153. ASSEC minutes March 1940.
154. ASSC minutes 30 March 1940.
155. ASSEC minutes 26 April 1940.
156. ASSC minutes 27 June 1940.
157. ASSC minutes 28 March 1941. See Croucher (1982) *Engineers*, pp. 99–100 for information on West of Scotland Shop Stewards Committee.
158. Croucher (1982) *Engineers*, pp. 188–189.
159. Ibid. pp. 228–229; also see pp. 285–294 regarding CWC activities.
160. Ibid. pp. 240–244 regarding Regulation 1A.A
161. AEU:GDC minutes 12 May 1944.
162. AEU:GDC minutes 29 April 1944.
163. McLaine *Ministry of Morale*, pp. 190–192.
164. Jeffreys *Story of*, p. 251.
165. ASSC minutes 17 January 1942.
166. Receipt from Glasgow Trades Council, 31 January 1942.
167. ASSC minutes 26 December 1941.
168. Quoted in Mark Stephens, *Ernest Bevin: Unskilled Labourer and World Statesman 1881–1951* (T&GWU, 1981), p. 97.
169. H A Clegg and Rex Adams, *The Employers' Challenge: A Study of the National Shipbuilding and Engineering Dispute of 1957*, (Blackwell, 1958), p. 158.
170. Croucher (1978) p. 318.
171. Hinton (1980) pp. 99–103.
172. Harry McShane and Joan Smith *No Mean Fighter* (Pluto Press, 1978), p. 236.
173. Duncan Hallas, who as a Manchester engineering apprentice joined the Workers International League in the Autumn of 1943, confirms that the WIL were able to work with 'craftist' engineering workers in many such situations. Interview with authors, 25 October 1993.
174. Clegg and Adams, *Employers' Challenge* 158–159.

Peter Bain works in the Department of Human Resource Management, University of Strathclyde. Tommy Gorman was for a number of years a senior shop steward and convenor at Albion Motors. He is currently a mature student at Glasgow Caledonian University.

THE SECOND WORLD WAR AND STALIN

Dave Morgan

MANY WHO WERE IN the army during the Second World War (as I was from September 1939 to November 1945) remember the a turning point of the war, and turning point of world history, when Hitler attacked the Soviet Union in 1941. For many soldiers it was eye-opening to see that the Red Army was the first to stop Hitler's armies in their tracks, to halt them at the gates of Leningrad and Moscow. Just at the time when the Army Bureau of Current Affairs revived the Cromwellian idea of an army that knew what it fought for and loved what it knew, British soldiers were asking why the Red Army was so successful: what was so different about this army? And they asked, too, what was different about the Soviet Union. In many parts of the army, they went on to ask about Communism. In my own unit, in that spring of 1942, we held a debate in which I moved the motion: 'That this house would prefer Communism to Capitalism after the war in Britain' (the wording was carefully checked by the Education Officer to make sure it did not contravene King's Regulations, and the voting was 66 for and 4 against.

The admiration for the Soviet Union was expressed in the slogan 'Joe for King!' and Uncle Joe (Stalin) was the hero of the whole army. After the war it took the concentrated efforts of the mass media to turn these feelings around and win support for the anti-Soviet aim of the Cold War. But in 1945 this was not yet achieved, and the Labour Party won its greatest parliamentary victory with a manifesto that said, 'The Labour Party is a socialist party, and proud of it'.

In 1945, too, Churchill recognised publicly that it was the Red Army which had pulverised Hitler's *Wehrmacht*. And for the achievements of the Red army many of us on the left gave the credit to Stalin. Even after the disclosures of the 20th Congress of the CPSU in February 1956 and the further information disclosed in the 1980s, many on the left felt uncomfortable about judging Stalin, even refusing to accept the evidence now available.

A historical judgement is still problematic, though the ongoing work towards an analysis must include the results of the autocratic and over-centralised system developed by Stalin, not only for the Soviet Union but imposed on other socialist countries after 1945, which alienated so many people that most socialist countries collapsed without a fight in 1989–90.

❏ Assessing Stalin

Much historical work on Stalin has been summed up in Alec Nove's book, *Stalinism and After*.[1] Much more briefly, the Congress resolution of the Communist Party of Britain (CPB), *Assessing the Collapse of the Soviet Union*, was an excellent definition of the nature of Stalinism without even mentioning the word Stalin[2], a curious contradiction which was questioned in advance by Max Adereth in his posthumously published study of British Communism and its revolutionary strategy, *Line of March*.[3]

Other valuable contributions on this subject have been made by Jean Elleinstein in *The Stalin Phenomenon*,[4] Anna Louise Strong in *The Stalin Era*[5] and Isaac Deutscher in *Stalin*.[6]

A little pamphlet by Joe Slovo, *Has Socialism Failed?*, published only two months after the Berlin wall came down, is remarkable for this clear definition: 'The term "Stalinism" is used to denote the bureaucratic authoritarian style of leadership (of parties both in and out of power) which denuded the party and the practice of socialism of most of its democratic content and concentrated power in the hands of a tiny, self-perpetuating elite'.[7]

Another source is *Let History Judge* by Roy Medvedev, a massive work packed with detailed information from which readers are left to draw their own analysis.[8]

As a necessary background to the war itself, the show trials of the 1930s must be seen as partly the result of the capitalist encirclement of the Soviet Union, promoting the 'siege mentality' in that country, and partly an expression of the autocratic and suspicious personality of Stalin himself. Much relevant material is to be found in biographies and autobiographies, such as that of Gromyko, in which he wrote:

> Staff at the Foreign Ministry did not discuss the purge trials of the 1930s, as diplomats we avoided the subject ... When I piece together what I know about Vyshinski (chief prosecutor) during the Stalin period and the trials of the so-called 'enemies of the people', I come to the conclusion that Vyshinski could not have been a true communist, but that he was a left-over from an alien political world. He had once been an active Menshevik and in the

summer of 1917 had been involved in the Provisional Government's search for Lenin, who was hiding in Finland ... he was a careerist without honour or conscience. Stalin obviously needed him for his own power-seeking purposes; he used Vyshinski to create the semblance of legal process in order to cover up the criminality of his mass repressions.[9]

With testimony from such old Bolsheviks as Gromyko there is no basis for suggesting that criticism of Stalin is a bourgeois phenomenon.

❑ Stalin and the War

On the war years, much has been written by former generals in the Red Army, as well as by Russian politicians and historians. But before coming to the war, we have to note that the leadership of the Red Army had been decimated in 1937 by the execution of Tukhachevsky, outstanding leader of the Red Army, together with two of the four other Marshals, 13 out of 15 senior Army Commanders, 50 out of 57 Corps Commanders, 14 out of 186 Divisional Commanders – altogether an estimated 25 per cent of the officers, who had to be replaced and trained at short notice. This was only four years before Hitler's attack; Zhukov, wartime leader of the Red Army, wrote in his autobiography:

> All the more unnatural, wholly out of gear with the substance of our system, and contrary to the situation in the country in 1937, were the unfounded arrests in the armed forces that year in contravention of socialist legality ... Prominent military leaders were arrested, which naturally affected the development of our armed forces and their combat preparedness.[10]

The word 'unfounded' shows the hollowness of the claim that Stalin's terror was aimed at traitors or opponents.

This repression was justified by allegations of a Nazi Fifth Column inside the Red Army, but no evidence for this has ever been found. Even at the Nuremberg trial of war criminals (1946), when the archives of the Nazi government were displayed, no word was found of any links with Red Army leaders. Only emotional and subjective reasons lie behind the reluctance of so many on the left to accept the evidence of Stalin's terror against many political and military leaders.

The second relevant point on Stalin's war record, after this vital decimation of the Red Army leadership, is his personal trust in the pact he made with Hitler in August 1939, a trust that remained right up to the attack on the Soviet Union in June 1941. This faith in Hitler's peaceful intentions was in spite of all the warnings of German military preparations given by diplomatic and political sources, as well as by military intelligence – outstandingly from Richard Sorge, their top agent in Japan.

The result of this faith was not only the complete surprise of the dawn attack by Hitler's forces (one example: about 1000 planes destroyed on the ground before they could even take off), but the bewilderment of Stalin himself at Hitler's 'perfidy'. He left Molotov to tell the people that war had begun and said no word in public until 3 July, twelve days after the attack on the Soviet Union. That period of silence has never been satisfactorily explained. But the first result, the complete surprise of Hitler's attack, combined with the unpreparedness of Soviet forces, led to the rapid advance of the Germans up to the gates of Moscow and Leningrad. Was that inevitable?

During the war, to summarise the available evidence, Stalin increasingly accepted the advice of his generals, developing a collective leadership which became more effective as the war went on. The final victory was won by the Red Army, with its high morale and patriotic inspiration, led by outstanding generals such as Zhukov. Alec Nove commented:

> There are those who say that the victory proves the basic correctness of the whole Stalinist line: collectivisation, industrial growth, the destruction of the opposition. I heard one such argue that the results of the battle of Stalingrad proves that Stalin's policies were right. A critic retorted, 'For all we know, but for Stalin's policies the Germans would not have got as far as Stalingrad'.[11]

❏ In the aftermath

After the war, millions of returning prisoners of war and civilians who had suffered under German occupation were treated as traitors and sent to internment camps. They were only officially declared innocent victims in January 1995. They had suffered from Stalin's usual method of mass condemnation by categories, e.g. his treatment of the Volga

Germans and of families or friends of individuals sentenced in the rigged trials of the 1930s (mostly later rehabilitated, even if posthumously).

A longer chapter would be needed to record the export of the Stalinist system to the new socialist countries after 1945, which has been documented and analysed by historians of the former German Democratic Republic. Although the Communist International had been ended in 1943, the control of other Communist Parties was enforced by the occupation of the Red Army in Eastern Europe, and especially by the security forces of the Soviet Union. The trials of leading Communists in Poland, Czechoslovakia and Hungary (around 150) were one blatant result; the excommunication of Yugoslavia was another.

In the GDR leaders like Walter Ulbricht had won the full trust of Moscow in their exile there during the war and so were able to prevent the murder of leading cadres seen in other neighbouring socialist countries, though there were purges in the GDR and the imprisonment of a number of innocent victims.

The exposure of Stalin's methods and crimes did not come, for most communists, until February 1956, when Khrushchev made his 'secret report' at a closed-session of the 20th Congress of the CPSU. But already there were books like Isaac Deutscher's *Stalin* which analysed the phenomenon of Stalinism. The first edition summed up Stalin as follows:

> What appears to be established is that Stalin belongs to the breed of the great revolutionary despots, to which Cromwell, Robespierre and Napoleon belonged. ... Finally, his inhuman despotism has not only vitiated much of his achievement – it may yet provoke a violent reaction against it, in which may be prone to forget, for a time, what it is they react against: the tyranny of Stalinism or its progressive social performance.[12]

These last lines (from 'it may yet ... ') are a remarkable forecast of what happened in fact to the Stalinist system in Eastern Europe in 1989–90. So much has been written about the end of the socialist countries, the end of a system that has been summed up in the word Stalinism, that one quotation may suffice to round this account off. It comes from Gromyko's autobiography:

> Stalin will provoke controversy for decades, if not centuries. A man of large calibre, he successfully held the Communist Party together

after Lenin's death and for a further thirty years played a determining role as the leader of a great power facing momentous tasks. Red Army men and partisans died with his name on their lips.

However, it would be wrong to see only his positive side, since he was a tragically contradictory figure. On the one hand, he was a man of powerful intellect, a leader with the unshakeable determination of the revolutionary, and also the ability to find common understanding with our wartime allies. On the other hand, he was a harsh man who did not count the human cost of achieving his aims, and who created a monstrously arbitrary state machine that sent multitudes of innocent Soviet people to their deaths. But this should not be allowed to overshadow our nation's achievements, in both war and peace. These achievements are great, and they were accomplished despite Stalin's monstrous crimes.[13]

Dave Morgan lived for many years in the former-GDR. He is a regular contributor to Socialist History.

NOTES

1. Alec Nove, *Stalinism and After* (Unwin Hyman, 1975).
2. *Assessing the Collapse of the Soviet Union* (CPB, 1993).
3. Max Adereth, *Line of March* (Praxis Press, 1994), pp. 49–50.
4. Jean Elleinstein, *The Stalin Phenomenon*, English translation (Lawrence and Wishart, 1976).
5. Anna Louise Strong, *The Stalin Era* (Mainstream, 1956).
6. Isaac Deutscher, *Stalin* (Penguin, 1949, 1990).
7. Joe Slovo, *Has Socialism Failed?* (Inkululeko Publications, 1990).
8. Roy Medvedev, *Let History Judge* (Oxford University Press, 1988).
9. Andrei Andrevich Gromyko, *Memories* (Arrow Books, 1989).
10. G. Zhukov, *Reminiscences and Reflections* (Progress Publishers, n.d.), p. 171.
11. Nove, *Stalinism*, p. 95.
12. Deutscher, *Stalin*, pp. 550–1 (1990 edition).
13. Gromyko, *Memories*, pp. 133–4.

Part Two: Christianity and Socialism
THE GRACE OF ALLIANCE

Chris Bryant

BY ITS VERY NATURE Christian Socialism is radical. It argues from the roots (Latin *radices*) of Christian faith. It seeks to make clear the essential elements of the teachings of Jesus. It reasserts what it sees as the earliest of Christian traditions. It posits fundamental truths. In many instances it wants to tear up by the roots what presently passes for theology and politics. It believes in change, both in its necessity and in its possibility. In the words of Tony Blair, 'To radicals (Christianity) has always had an especial validity. Radicals want change, and change, both personal and social, lies at the heart of the Christian religion'.

It is because of the radical nature of Christian Socialism that it is vital, in order fully to understand the present day phenomenon of Christian Socialism, to gain at least a cursory understanding of the theological tradition to which the Christian Socialists refer. This requires a brief glimpse at the main elements of the Judaeo–Christian biblical tradition, embracing both the theological history of the Israelites up to the birth of Jesus of Nazareth, and the accounts of Jesus's own teachings; a look at the early church as annalled in some of the New Testament writings, and through into the third and fourth centuries, when the canon of Christian theology was being fixed; and a short analysis of the essential Christian doctrines from which the Christian Socialists derive their beliefs. We shall then progress to the modern history of Christian Socialism, focusing primarily on its British manifestations, from the history of the Levellers and Diggers through to the Christian Socialist Movement and the election of Tony Blair as the second Christian Socialist Labour Leader in a row.

❏ The biblical history of Israel

The books which constitute the Old Testament, written across a period of more than a thousand years, have always been upheld by Christian Socialists as harbouring the earliest and clearest examples of an understanding of society and of the political endeavour that should inform our dealings in every age. Both the narrative of a people sold into slavery in Egypt and released by a God that led them into a Promised Land and the political precepts of that society point to some of the key ideas of Christian Socialism.

Thus the Torah, which embodies the Mosaic Law, enunciates a clear understanding of what God (Yahweh) requires of the people. Firstly, the land is not to be regarded as private property because it belongs to the God (Yahweh) who created it, and is a common treasury. It is apportioned equally to tribes and peoples, but 'Land shall not be sold absolutely, for the land belongs to me, and you are only strangers and guests of mine' (Leviticus 25.23). Furthermore usury, the lending of money at interest, is expressly forbidden, 'If you lend money to any of my people, to anyone poor among you, you will not play the usurer with him; you will not demand interest from him' (Exodus 22.24). The clear imperative to generosity within the community is then further connected with this prohibition: 'If your brother becomes impoverished and cannot support himself in the community, you will assist him as you would a stranger or a guest, so that he can go on living with you. Do not charge him interest on a loan, but fear your God, and let your brother live with you. You will not lend him money on interest or give him food to make a profit out of it' (Leviticus 25.35–7).

Furthermore the Law goes on to specify the prevention of poverty as a core aim of the community. 'At the end of every seven years, you must grant remission. The nature of the remission is as follows: any creditor holding a personal pledge obtained from his fellow must release him from it ... There must, then, be no poor among you' (Deuteronomy 15.1–3). This seventh year of remission is made every seventh time into the year of Jubilee with liberty for all slaves and prisoners, a redistribution of land, the end of debt and a fresh start for all (Leviticus 25).

The most vulnerable are also protected under specific statute: 'If, when reaping the harvest in your field, you overlook a sheaf in that field, do not go back for it. The foreigner, the orphan and the widow shall have it, so that Yahweh your God may bless you in all your undertakings' (Deuteronomy 24.19). Debt-collecting from the poor must be without forced entry, wages are to be paid before the end of the day, and the means of making a living can never be taken to redeem a debt (Deuteronomy 24). Finally, the legal system must be impartial, 'You will not be unjust in administering justice. You will neither be partial to the poor nor overawed by the great' (Leviticus 19.15).

Indeed the story of the Exodus shows that God, in his very nature, has a preferential option for the poor and the vulnerable. He hears their cries in Egypt, he hears the cries of the wages of the poor, he

THE GRACE OF ALLIANCE

hears the cries of the oppressed. The very nature of the God Yahweh is that he is a God of justice and of peace.

It is from this core theological law then that the whole of the later works of the Old Testament derive their understanding. The Exodus narrative, starting in the injustice of Joseph being sold into slavery, through to the brickmakers' strike and Moses leading the slaves into freedom, fixes in the minds of the people a historic identity that clearly unites them and binds them to the stranger, the widow and the orphan, as well as 'the poor of the land'.

It is into this tradition that both the judges and the Prophets speak with remarkable clarity. Thus the judge Samuel is fiercely against the institution of a monarchy, though he later bends to the will of the people, and much of the Wisdom literature is written to condemn any understanding of divine retribution that might lead to the belief that the rich are those blessed by God because they have been good. The prophets go much further, condemning those who are more interested in worship than in justice: 'Is not this the kind of fasting that pleases me: to break unjust fetters, to undo the thongs of the yoke, to let the oppressed go free, and to break all yokes? Is it not sharing your food with the hungry, and sheltering the homeless poor?' (Isaiah 58.6). They champion the poor, attacking the society that allows the poor to be sold for a pair of sandals (Amos 2.6), and demanding of politicians that they do likewise (Jeremiah 22.1). The epitome of injustice becomes the unjust use of power to dispossess the poor, as in the tale of Naboth's Vineyard.

Within the prophetic writing there develops too an identifiable vision of the ideal society, partly recognisable already, but mostly to be striven for. The frustration of this vision is then translated into the hope of a messianic Kingdom of God that will be worldwide, will issue in a reign of justice, and will signal peace. Especially in the turbulent period leading up to the birth of Jesus, the expectation of a Davidic King grew with a revolutionary zeal informed by the experience of occupation and manifest injustice.

❏ The accounts of Jesus's teaching

It is this tradition then that Jesus learns from his earliest days, and it is only in the context of this tradition that the accounts of Jesus's teachings make sense. Thus for the writer of Luke's gospel the concept of the year of remission and of Jubilee is the core teaching, and Jesus recites the Jubilee text at his first meeting in the synagogue, 'The Spirit of the Lord is upon me, for he has anointed me to bring good news to the afflicted. He has sent me to proclaim liberty to the captives, sight to the blind, to let the oppressed go free, to proclaim a year of favour from the Lord' (Luke 4.18–19 and Isaiah 61.1–2). Jesus's message is clearly political, and its key themes are the same as those of the Jewish Law. There is again a preferential option for the poor, clearly expressed in the Beatitudes, 'Blessed are you poor' (Luke 6.20), and those who thirst after justice are also to be counted amongst the blessed. The division between the sheep and the goats is not by their religious allegiance, but by whether they have fed the poor, clothed the naked and visited those in prison. It will be more difficult for the rich to enter the Kingdom of Heaven than for a camel to pass through the eye of a needle. Generosity, not only to those whom we know, but even to the Samaritan, is a central part of the response to God. At his conception Mary sings a 'song of high revolt' in which she praises the Almighty for 'he has pulled down princes from their thrones and raised high the lowly. He has filled the hungry with good things, and has sent the rich away empty' (Luke 1.52–3). In the story of the rich man and the beggar Lazarus at his gate, Abraham despairs of the rich man's friends' ability to repent of their hardness of heart towards the poor even if someone should come from the dead to persuade them. The money-changers in the Temple are cast out for turning the House of God into a robbers' den.

In all the teachings of Jesus then, or, more importantly, in the authors' accounts of those teachings, there is a clear expectation of a political implication to the new Kingdom that is embodied in Jesus. Indeed in Luke's account, which also forms the first half of a two-volume history embracing The Acts of the Apostles, the whole structure of the account centres around the development of the new community which is the Church, and all its social and political implications.

It is also, of course, important at this point to note that the supposedly historical accounts of the three synoptic gospels (Matthew, Mark and Luke), form a very different basis to Christian Socialism from that of the more apparently theological John. Yet the doctrine of the Incarnation, the belief that 'The Word became flesh', which opens John, has been just as significant an element of the Christian Socialist theological resource.

❏ The early church

Luke's account of the early church is absolutely unambiguous, 'And all who shared the faith owned everything in common; they sold their goods and possessions and distributed the proceeds among themselves according to what each one needed' (Acts 2.44). The social implications of Christian faith are from the outset then made not an added extra, but a core part of being faithful. The epistle of James argues ferociously into the specifics of a new Christian community, 'My brothers, do not let class distinction enter into your faith in Jesus Christ, our glorified Lord ... it was those who were poor according to the world that God chose, to be rich in faith and to be the heirs to the kingdom which he promised to those who love him. You, on the other hand, have dishonoured the poor' (James 2.1, 5–6). Again generosity is of the very nature of Christian living, for faith without deeds is dead.

And it has to be emphasised that the history of the church into the third and fourth centuries provides a unanimous witness to the core practice of common ownership and the need to make very special provision for the poor. Justin argued 'Do you therefore, O bishops, be solicitous about their maintenance, being in nothing wanting to them; ... to the strangers, an house; to the hungry, food; to the thirsty, drink; to the naked, clothing; to the sick, visitation; to the prisoners, visitation' (Apostolic Constitutions). This could, of course, be simply dismissed as so much charity, except for Charles Gore's understanding:

> The teaching of Jesus about the worth of each individual, the poorest and the weakest, expressed itself in the Christian idea of brotherhood, and the institution of the Church as a body in which 'if one member suffer, all the members suffer with it'. This idea and this institution carried with it a doctrine of property, which echoed our Lord's strong disparagement of wealth, and was in theory and practice highly communal. The Christians were a persecuted body, who had no power of controlling the law or practice of the society of the Empire; but within their own 'voluntary' society the claim of the brethren was paramount ... There is no doubt that this profound sense of the communal claim on private property and this practically effective sense of brotherhood produced an economic condition in the Christian community which was one main cause of its progress'.[1]

Furthermore the early theologians universally taught that humanity was, by its very nature, social. Cyprian extended this even to prayer: 'Above all things, the Teacher of Peace and the Master of Unity is unwilling that prayer should be made separately and privately, each man when he prays praying for himself alone. Our prayer is public and common, and when we pray, we pray not for one man, but for the whole people, for with us the whole people is one'.[2]

In the fourth century all four great Greek doctors, Athanasius, Basil, Gregory of Nazianzus and John Chrysostom, argued from a fundamentally social understanding of property.

> Tell me then, whence art thou rich? From whom didst thou receive it, and from whom he that hath transmitted it to thee? From his father and his grandfather. But canst thou, ascending through may generations, show the acquisition just? It cannot be. The root and origin of it must be injustice. Why? Because God in the beginning made not one man rich and another poor. Nor did he afterwards take and show to one treasures of gold, and deny to the other the right of searching for it: but he left the earth free to all alike. Why then if it is common, have you so many acres of land, whilst your neighbour has not a portion of it?[3]

And the four great Latin fathers, Ambrose, Augustine of Hippo, Jerome and Gregory the Great, all railed too: 'How far, ye rich men, will your mad greed be strained? Will you dwell quite alone on the earth? Why do you cast out what is natural and usurp the ownership of nature? Nature knows no rich men, she made us all poor'.[4]

Thus, by the end of the fourth century the following ideas had become essential elements of the theological canon:

1. Our humanity is social by its very nature, and any political system has to recognise that social-ism and work with the grain of it. 'According to the will of God and natural origin, it is our business to work in the mutual aid of another ... to aim in our various callings, for example, to make all advantages common profit, and in scriptural language to be helpmeets to one another, whether we do this by study in our calling, by money, or by any other means that the grace of alliance may increase in our midst'.[5]

2. Injustice is contrary to the will of God, and its most common feature is a sharp divide between rich and poor, which is the

inevitable result of an unbridled acquisitiveness on behalf of the powerful. In particular usury is an act of unfaithfulness.
3. The Church at least must be a mirror of righteousness: 'the embodied form of justice, all men's common right. She prays in common, she works in common, and she possesses in common'.[6]
4. The doctrine of the incarnation means that Christian faith is not aimed at some other world, but is deeply concerned about the lives we live in this one.
5. The created world is to be considered as a 'common treasury' which is to be stewarded by humanity for the good of all. Private property is either to be relinquished for the common good, or at least treated without any ultimate possessiveness.
6. The nature of God is social, expressed in the Trinity. God is known in justice and in peace, and in sacrificial generosity.
7. All humanity is made in the image of God, and therefore all humans must be considered equal.

Clearly it would then be beyond the scope of an article such as this to delineate the full ecclesiastical history of the middle ages and the transformation of a Christian orthodoxy that rejected usury into one that espoused capitalism. That work was done more than ably by R H Tawney in *Religion and the Rise of Capitalism*.[7] Of course the radical tradition continued, as the life of Joachim of Fiore (1145–1202), the Poor Men of Lyons under Peter Waldo, the weavers' revolt led by Thomas Munzer (1490–1526), and the Anabaptist tradition show, but it is impossible to understand the real experiences of the nineteenth-century Christian Socialists without a perception that they fundamentally believed that the Christian gospel had been drastically altered, and that their true aim was to revitalise the real, original and radical gospel.

❑ The Levellers, Laud, and others

In Britain the radical tradition rarely disappeared. Thus the radical priest John Ball accompanied Wat Tyler in the first great poll tax revolts in 1381 and preached against Richard II in 1381 on the text 'When Adam dalf and Eve span/Who was then the gentleman?'.

Yet it was in the seventeenth century that the flowering of what might first be termed genuine Christian Socialism occurred. Archbishop

William Laud was being accused of being a 'very seditious fellow' in 1620 for preaching against the enclosures, and could hold no truck with economic individualism: 'If any man be so addicted to his private, that he neglect the common state, he is void of the sense of piety and wisheth peace and happiness to himself in vain'.[8] The Bishop of Winchester, Lancelot Andrewes, preached constantly against the sin of usury, and in 1631 the Reverend Peter Simon was preaching the equality of all mankind in the Forest of Dean.

Most importantly, however, later in the seventeenth century and in the midst of the theological melee that was the English Civil War, the Levellers, and their extreme wing, the True Levellers or Diggers, came to the fore. Thus in 1648 a group of Levellers published *A Light shining in Buckinghamshire* which called for 'a just portion for each man to live so that none need to beg or steal for want but that every man may live comfortably' and 'a just rule for each man to go by, which rule is to be the Scriptures'. It also called for government by 'Judges called Elders', to be elected by the people, and for the confiscation of bishops' lands and Crown properties to provide a public fund for the maintenance of the needy. All this was to inaugurate a commonwealth 'after the pattern of the Bible in which the land would be the common property of all'. The main adherents, Lilburne and Walwyn, argued provocatively with both Fairfax and Cromwell, and from 1648 to 1649 produced a regular journal, *The Moderate,* which was finally banned by Parliament in September.

In 1649, the year of Charles' execution, on April 1, a merchant taylor originally from Wigan called Gerard Winstanley and a few others took the Levellers' cause further and moved to St George's Hill, Cobham in Surrey and started to dig up the common land. It was an experiment founded in Winstanley's deep Christian conviction that Christ had ushered in a 'New Law', and that men and women were called to live in common society. The New Jerusalem was not 'to be seen only hereafter', but to be 'seen and known within creation, and the blessing shall spread within all nations'.[9] God is not distant, but is to be found in the lives and experiences of ordinary men and women. The spirit of prophecy from the Old Testament is still alive, and society will be called to account, for the second coming of Christ is the start of a new age of community. Violence was not to be met with violence, for the New Law enjoined peace. Winstanley attacked the religious intolerance of the established church, the continuance of tithing, the arbitrary nature of most legal decisions, and the lack of change under Cromwell's Commonwealth. He advocated annual local elections, for 'nature tells us that if water stands long it corrupts; whereas running water keeps sweet and is fit for the common use'.[10] Education was to be the right of all, with public schools teaching science and a trade to all, with no one section of children set aside as 'academics'. Buying and selling within the community was to be outlawed as the source of all warring, and gold to be used for foreign trade.

The utopia that Winstanley espoused, however, and the experiment of Cobham, lasted little more than a year. For the local landowners, with the support of Parliament, drove the Diggers' cattle off the land, and a savage period of harassment led to the dissolution of the community at Easter in 1650. The Diggers attempted to resettle elsewhere without success, but Winstanley went on to write extensively, enumerating the popular grievances of the times and arguing for a 'True Commonwealth' with no buying and selling which 'did bring in, and still doth bring in discontents and wars'. Equality, justice, peace, cooperation are the keystones of Winstanley's writings within a clearly theological setting:

> This great Leveller, Christ our King of Righteousness in us, shall cause men to beat their swords into ploughshares and spears into pruning hooks, and nations shall learn war no more; and every one shall delight to let each other enjoy the pleasures of the earth, and shall hold each other no longer in bondage.[11]

At the same time as the Levellers and Diggers, the Quakers were reforming Christian understandings of the body politic. Following in the traditions of the Anabaptists, the early Quakers held a strong belief in the power of the 'inner light' as opposed to the received wisdoms of tradition. Named also the Society of Friends after 3 John 1.14: 'Our friends salute thee; greet the friends by name', the Quakers spent much of the seventeenth century under persecution: between 1651 and 1656 1900 Quakers were imprisoned in England. George Fox, the son of a Leicestershire silk weaver, founded the movement with its particular brand of rationalism, mysticism, democracy and political abstention, arguing for a complete repudiation of war and forcible resistance to violence, the doctrine of equal respect to all and a refusal to take oaths. Fox fulminated against the rich, called for common ownership of the land, and expected that the new era of God's reign would only start when all England recognised the 'inner light' within them.

The Quakers also attracted many from Cromwell's army, men like the ex-quartermaster James Naylor who was imprisoned in 1652 for blasphemy and later tried before the Bar of the House of Commons. Most significantly the interrelation of politics and theology meant that the vast majority of Quakers were tried for theological rather than political dissent, for it was the basis upon which they preached as much as the conclusions they came to.

The most important of the Quakers was undoubtedly John Bellers, whom Marx referred to as 'a phenomenal figure in the history of political economy'.[12] In 1695 Bellers wrote an essay entitled *Proposals for raising a college of industry of all useful trades and husbandry with Profit for the Rich, a plentiful living for the Poor and a good education for Youth, which will be advantage to the government by the Increase of the People and their riches. Motto: Industry brings Plenty – The Sluggard shall be clothed with Rags. He that will not work shall not eat.* In it he advocated a communal colony where value would be measured not in terms of money, but in units of labour-time. Though Sir William Petty had already in 1662 recognised the principle, Bellers was the first person to argue for it being put into practice, anticipating Robert Owen by more than a century.

The history of anything approaching Christian Socialism throughout the seventeenth century lies mostly with a series of smaller sects and dissenting groups, culminating perhaps most notably in the complicated figure of William Blake, who has regularly been claimed by antinomians, Swedenborgians and a vast array of others. What remains clear is that he had a radical understanding of the Bible, refusing to accept anything but the rule of the Spirit. He also fervently expected the ushering in of a new historical era when Jerusalem shall be built 'among these dark satanic mills', and believed that politics and religion were the same thing.

With the beginning of the nineteenth century and the onset of the more advanced results of the Industrial Revolution, social understandings became increasingly divided. The landed gentry, at least until the Reform Act of 1832, had a clear monopoly of government, and even then the franchise was not extended to the town worker (until 1867) or the village labourer (1884). Furthermore the Combination Acts forbade the formation of trade unions. Even after the Acts' repeal in 1825, six labourers from Tolpuddle, Dorset, were transported for seven years in 1834 for combining to raise their wages. The Tolpuddle Martyrs, led by a Methodist local preacher, George Loveless, and supported in the main by radical church people like the Vicar of Warwick, Dr Wade, became an early focus in the Chartist and Christian Socialist movements, but the great sweep of history presented a theological understanding vastly different from the early Church. The Age of Enlightenment had made of God a distant clockmaker who had set the world in motion but was not much more involved. The poor were to be pitied as the objects of charity rather than emancipated. Even the great philanthropists of the early nineteenth century taught the poor to suffer their present afflictions silently, for there was a greater reward in heaven. Thus William Wilberforce and Hannah More all sought greater moral instruction as the answer to the ills of the time. Hannah More addressed the women of Shipham: 'Let me remind you that probably that very scarcity had been permitted by an all-wise and gracious Providence to unite all ranks of people together, to show the poor how immediately they are dependent upon the rich and to show both rich and poor that they are all dependent on Himself'. Even those involved in leading the Ten Hours Bill Movement, such as the Earl of Shaftesbury, were by no means radical: 'all should be carried out in a most conciliatory manner, that there should be a careful abstinence from all approach to questions of wages and capital'.

At the same time the Methodists were finding a rich vein of religious expression amongst those disillusioned with the established church. Methodism grew rapidly throughout the land, and the 1818 Act of Parliament that gave millions of pounds to the building of inner city churches was partly justified on the grounds that it would be unwise to leave the industrial belt of Britain to the affections of the Methodists. Yet it is vital to point out at this stage that much of early nineteenth-century Methodism was not in any sense socialist. Indeed most Methodist sermons of the day reiterated the gospel of a fair reward for the deserving poor at the end of time. Cobbett argued in *The Political Register* of 12 June 1813: 'There are, I know, persons who look upon the Methodists ... as *friends of freedom*. It is impossible they should be'. Yet Methodism played a vital role in the development of a radical social understanding, for every Methodist chapel was a school that taught reading and writing, enabled people to speak and learn to express themselves. The fire of the Old Testament prophets mixed with the social conditions of the poor who attended Chapel rather than Church meant that it soon became inevitable that many Methodists would become prominent in the movements for political change.

Thus many of the first Co-operators, the Rochdale Pioneers, were associated with the Cookite Methodists of the Clover Street Chapel, most notably James Wilkinson, the shoemaker preacher known as 'The Reverend'.

Most significantly in the 1830s, the large part of the opposition to the Poor Law of 1834 came from those who believed it offended against Biblical principles. Richard Oastler and Joseph Stephens, both ministers, argued solely from a Christian position, comparing the Poor Law Commissioners and Malthus to Herod who had ordered the massacre of the innocents. At a meeting in Newcastle in 1838 Stephens called for the Act's repeal, warning that otherwise the people should rise up, and 'if all failed, then the firebrand – aye, the firebrand, I repeat'.[13]

Finally it is important at this stage to recognise the significant theological changes that the early nineteenth century witnessed. Romanticism, especially through the work of Coleridge, had increasingly come to speak of an immanent God, which started to make a renewed sense of Incarnationalism. Furthermore theologians increasingly questioned the straight historicity of the Biblical accounts of Jesus's life. The search for the historical Jesus focused attention on the teachings and the context of Jesus's life as much as the theological interpretation of it, and the new science of archaeology brought many more facets of the Old Testament writings into question. At the same time the divide between, in Disraeli's words, 'the two nations' of rich and poor became the subject of constant Church debate as the established church's universal parish system was stretched to its limits. Issues of ritualism and the relation of the Church and State were sharply highlighted by the Repression of Bishoprics in Ireland, and several prominent clergy joined the Roman Catholic Church.

❑ The modern history of Christian Socialism

C B Dunn, the curate of Cumberworth, and John Rabine of Birmingham, both prominent Co-operators, first used the phrase 'Christian Socialists' in 1837, but those looking for a clear starting date for modern Christian Socialism, have normally looked to 1848. For on 4 April the National Convention of Chartists in London had decided to present their great petition to Parliament on 10 April. On this date the Revd Charles Kingsley, the Rector of Eversley in Hampshire, with a letter of introduction from another Anglican clergyman, Frederick Dennison Maurice, turned up at the office of

John Ludlow, another friend of Maurice's. The two men went to the Chartist rally on Kennington Common, only to find that rain and little enthusiasm had kept the Chartist numbers well below the 150,000 confidently expected, and feared by the authorities. By the end of the day they had returned to Maurice's house, and printed a first placard addressed to 'The WorkMen of England' and signed 'A Working Parson'. The following day they set up a new publication, to be known as *Politics for the People*. They were soon joined by Thomas Hughes, of *Tom Brown's Schooldays* fame, and the wealthy philanthropist Edward Vansittart Neale. What was clear was that Maurice, who was later in 1853 removed from his post at King's College, London, was the undoubted leader of the group. His theological depth of understanding and his intellectual commitment to the task of 'socialising Christianity and christianising socialism' was vital: 'Let us not try to sever, for they are inseparable, those principles which affect the problems of earth from those which affect the Kingdom of Heaven. All unrighteous government whatever, all that sets itself against the order and freedom of man, is hostile to Christ's government, is rebellious against him, in whatsoever name and by whatsoever instruments it is administered'.[14]

Charles Kingsley, the author of *The Water Babies*, *Alton Locke* and *Yeast*, was the one to popularise the movement through his vivid portrayal of the social conditions in the sweatshops of London and the debilitating oppression of poverty. Maurice was, however, the theological innovator of the group. 'I see it clearly. We must not beat about the bush ... What right have we to address the English people? We must have something special to tell them, or we ought not to speak. "Tracts on Christian Socialism" is, it seems to me, the only title which will define our object, and will commit us at once to the conflict we must engage in sooner or later with the unsocial Christians and the unchristian Socialist'.[15]

Ludlow, however, was the politician, with a clear agenda, and a determined understanding of what needed to be done, and what had to get onto the Statute book. Thus it was largely through his work that the Industrial and Provident Societies Act of 1852 came into force, enabling the fuller development of the Co-operative Movement.

What was distinctive about the contribution of these Christian Socialists was the integrity of the work. Thus practical work was to be integrated with theological consideration and with education. Henry Mayhew's *London Labour and the London Poor* made a dramatic impact in 1849 with its description of the sweatshops and living conditions of the London poor, and the Christian Socialists decided that the answer lay in the Co-operatives that they had heard of in France, for at first they knew nothing of the work of Robert Owen. They set about initiating a Tailors' Association, which was later followed by builders' and needleworkers' associations. Maurice wrote to Kingsley: 'Competition is put forward as the law of the universe. That is a lie. the time has come for us to declare that it is a lie by word and deed. I see no way but associating for work instead of for strikes.'[16] In 1850 the first edition of the *Christian Socialist* appeared, and a series of Tracts on Christian Socialism was launched. Kingsley wrote: 'We have used the Bible as if it were a mere special constable's handbook, an opium dose for keeping beasts of burden patient while they are being overloaded',[17] sustaining the attack on the theological as well as the economic principles of the day. Also in 1850 the Society for Promoting Working Men's Associations was established and the Christian Socialists set about the formation of associations of producers. In October, Neale put up the money for opening the first consumers' cooperative, The London Co-operative Stores at 76 Charlotte Street, which later became the Co-operative Wholesale Association.

Yet the Christian Socialists did not last beyond 1854 as an identifiable movement. The magazine and many of the other enterprises folded late in 1853, and by the Leeds Co-operative Conference of 1854 there is no specific contribution from the Christian Socialists. The work, however, continued. Thus Maurice, together with John Ruskin and Dante Gabriel Rossetti, founded the Working Men's College in Red Lion Square in 1853, and worked throughout the land for the Workers' Education Association, arguing in particular for women's education.

The early Christian Socialists could only sustain a six-year period of activity. But the radical tradition was inherited in a far more coherent form by a series of later organisations. In 1877 the Guild of St Matthew was founded in Bethnal Green by the Anglican priest Stewart Duckworth Headlam who had met Maurice at Cambridge. It was the first attempt to create a Socialist organisation, and though it came from a specifically Anglo-Catholic background, the work of Headlam spread far wider, later taking a significant part in the Fabian Society. He said, 'I have always deprecated other-worldliness, as it is called, a morbid concern about self, hysterical visions of Heaven, as though earth were a place to be despaired of. I have always talked of the Kingdom of Heaven being fulfilled here and now on earth, and deprecated too much dwelling on a future life, fortified by the fact that Christ Himself said very little about the other world, and very much about this'.[18] In 1884 the Guild called for 'such measures as will tend ... to bring about the better distribution of wealth created by labour'. Headlam was sacked by the Bishop of London, and spent much of his later life as a London County Councillor and member of the London School Board.

Contemporaneous with the Guild was the more moderate Christian Social Union which stopped short of socialism, but many of whose members were closely involved with the founding of the Labour Party. Bishop Brooke Foss Westcott, Henry Scott Holland, the editor of the *Commonwealth* and Bishop Charles Gore were the leading lights of a movement whose most significant contribution lay in the publication in 1889 of *Lux Mundi*, which preached a gospel firmly based in the Incarnation. 'Socialism is the opposite of Individualism', Westcott argued.

Similarly Roman Catholic teaching in Britain took a dramatic change late in the nineteenth century. Pope Leo XIII's encyclical *Rerum Novarum* of 1891 set out a clearly new attitude to work and to trade unions. Labour was no longer to be viewed simply as a part of the machinery, but work was a specifically human activity. Its remuneration could not then be made to depend solely on the state of the market, but 'must be determined by the laws on justice and equity'.[19]

❏ The Labour Party

With the formation of the new Labour Party and its first electoral successes, radical Christians were excited. Many saw the general election of 1906 as providing a genuinely prophetic opportunity. The Baptist leader John Clifford denounced those who claimed Christianity had nothing to say on the real matters of political equity as being guilty of 'flat paganism'. In 1907 the Community of the Resurrection at Mirfield invited Labour leaders and socialists to discuss social issues. Keir Hardie regularly thereafter shared platforms with the fathers from Mirfield.

Also in 1906 the Church Socialist League was founded, focusing primarily on Anglican clergy in Newcastle. It committed itself from the outset to 'the establishment of a democratic commonwealth in which the community shall own the land and capital and use them cooperatively for the good of all'.[20] Algernon West, James Adderley and Lewis Donaldson all saw in socialism a capacity to transform 'thoughtless and selfish and vicious lives'. In the 1907 Jarrow by-election the League worked hard for the socialist cause, returning the Independent Labour Party candidate Pete Curran. W E Moll, one of the League's leaders, was elected to the ILP administrative Council in 1907, and served for three years. The League's periodical, the *Christian Commonwealth* was clearly identified with the ILP, and had regular contributions from all the leading parliamentarians, as well as Annie Besant and Beatrice Webb. The League was, however, purely Anglican, and the work of Congregationalists like Frederick Swan in Colne Valley, had no organisational support or channel. The American Methodist J Stitt Wilson visited the West Riding in 1907 and preached socialism. In Halifax more than three hundred people joined the ILP following his crusade. In the Spring of 1908 the congregationalist R J Campbell founded the League of Progressive Religious and Social Thought in order 'to spiritualise the social movement of the age', and embraced Christian Socialism.

By the start of the First World War, then, Christian Socialism had become closely identified with the Labour Party. Keir Hardie saw his task as seeking to build a society on the precept of the ten commandments and the Sermon on the Mount, and many clergy, especially in the industrial concentrations of poverty, supported the task.

In 1918 one of the key members of the League, Fr Conrad Noel, was instrumental in setting up the Catholic Crusade, which sought to be more expressly socialist and Catholic. It welcomed the Russian Revolution, and finally split on the issue of Trotsky and Stalin, with the anti-Stalin group running the Order of the Church Militant. Noel, the 'Red Vicar of Thaxted', led the Catholic Crusade with the verve of a visionary, and argued a tight theological case for socialism, based on the incarnational doctrine from which his ritualism stemmed, as well as the 'social' doctrine of the Trinity. A small minority of the Church Socialist League then founded the Society of Socialist Christians, together with members of the Socialist Quaker Society and the Free Church Socialist League. Its newspaper, the *Crusader* was later renamed the *Christian Socialist*. In 1930 a group of MPs led a Christian Socialist Crusade, which merged with the Society of Socialist Christians to form the Socialist Christian League, with the support of the Labour Leader George Lansbury, who stated 'are we not taught that because Christ himself became flesh, therefore all life is sacred?'.[21]

❏ Archbishop Temple

The history of Christian Socialism in the first half of this century cannot, however, be told without reference to the one figure who refused to join all the socialist organisations, William Temple, the wartime Archbishop of Canterbury. Temple was himself the son of an Archbishop, and educated at Oxford. Closely involved with the Workers' Education Association, and briefly a member of the Labour Party, Temple was ordained in 1909, was Rector of St James, Piccadilly, founded the short-lived Life and Liberty Movement in 1917 and was made Bishop of Manchester in 1921. He served on the radical Church of England committee that had published *Christianity And Industrial Problems* in 1918, together with Gore, and George Lansbury and R H Tawney. The report argued that the fundamental evil of modern society was that it encouraged competition for private gain rather than cooperation for public service. It recommended the principle of a living wage, unemployment insurance and the setting up of an industrial parliament.

In 1924 Temple went on to bring together the Conference on Christian Politics, Economics and Citizenship (Copec) in Birmingham, which had a clearly Christian Socialist outlook. Maurice Reckitt and Ruth Kenyon of the League of the Kingdom of God attended, as did the pacifist Bishop of Chichester, George Bell. The reports of the conference argued that the first call on industry should be a decent living wage for the ordinary worker, not the interests of the shareholders; 'extremes of wealth and poverty are likewise intolerable. A Christian order involves a juster distribution'.[22] The tone of the conference was radical, but the issues were presented as much in individual terms as social ones: 'we feel there is a strong challenge to all Christians to work out a better standard of life which would not only in theory but in practice make better but less costly living more possible'.[23] The conference papers did not, however, lead to a significant change in society, nor to a continuing movement. The Christian Left was active, but primarily through other means, such as the Student Christian Movement, the new development agencies and some of the senior theological figures. Key amongst these were the Quaker Professor John MacMurray, with his advanced theories of the personal and the social, and Dr Hewlett Johnson, the Dean of Canterbury.

In 1941, however, Temple called a second meeting, at Malvern, which was attended by about 210 people, predominantly Anglican in church affiliation. Some were far from socialist, including the poet T S Eliot and the majority of the Christendom Group, but the tenor of the conference was again socialist. The aim of the conference 'was to consider from the Anglican point of view what are the fundamental facts which are directly relevant to the ordering of the new society that is evidently emerging, and how Christian thought can be shaped to play a leading part in the reconstruction after the war is over'.[24] Much of the debate at the conference was between Sir Richard Acland, the MP and founder of the Commonwealth Party, and others who found the condemnation of all private property impossible to advocate. The conference finally agreed 'that the maintenance of that part of the structure of our society, by which the ultimate ownership of the principal industrial resources of the community can be vested in the hands of private owners, may be ... a stumbling block ... contrary to divine justice, making it harder for men to live Christian lives.'[25] By June, 200,000 copies of a summary of the proceedings had been sold, and in 1942 Temple, by now Archbishop of York, published *Christianity and Social Order* which sold 140,000 copies in Penguin, and was largely based on the Malvern conference.

Temple's work is primarily concerned not with political solutions, but with how Christianity can contribute to the political task. He argues from a clearly incarnational view, 'Christianity is the most materialistic of the world's religions'. He asserted the need for three quintessential Christian political principles: freedom, fellowship and service, and he drew an important distinction between personality and individuality: 'Every person is an individual, but his individuality is what marks him off from others; it is a principle of division; whereas personality is social, and only in his social relationships can a man be a person ... This point has great political importance: for these relationships exists in the whole network of communities and associations and fellowships. It is in these that the real wealth of human life consists'.[26] Following from this then stems Temple's understanding of the need for a social society:

(1) Every child should find itself a member of a family housed with decency and dignity, so that it may grow up as a member of that basic community in a happy fellowship unspoilt by underfeeding or overcrowding, by dirty or drab surroundings or by mechanical monotony of environment.

(2) Every child should have the opportunity of an education till years of maturity, so planned as to allow for his peculiar aptitudes and make possible their full development'.[27]

The assessment of Temple's contribution to Christian Socialism is difficult. For John Atherton he is a Christian Liberal, yet for many he paved the way for much of the welfare state and the election of the Labour Party at the end of the Second World War.

❏ R H Tawney

The other key figure of this period is R H Tawney, the social historian who analysed the history of Christianity and Capitalism more keenly than any other, and worked within the Labour Party towards his vision based on equality: 'to criticise inequality and desire equality is not, as is sometimes suggested, to cherish the romantic illusion that people are equal in character and intelligence. It is to hold that, while their natural endowments differ profoundly, it is the mark of a civilised society to aim at eliminating such inequalities as have their source, not in individual differences, but in its own organisation, and that individual differences which are a source of social energy, are more like to ripen and find expression if social inequalities are, as far as practicable, diminished'.[28]

It was under Tawney's aegis that, on 20 January 1960, the Christian Socialist Movement brought together both the Socialist Christian League and the Society of Socialist Clergy, which had been founded after the Malvern conference as the Council of Clergy for Common Ownership. There was an informal manifesto, published on May Day 1959, signed by Tom Driberg, John Groser, Donald Soper, George MacLeod and Mervyn Stockwood amongst others, and entitled *Papers from the Lamb*. Its title came from the name of the Holborn pub where Driberg and others had met regularly to discuss their faith and politics, rather than from theology. As a manifesto, however, it was less concerned with practicalities than with ideals. As they say, 'these papers do not purport to give a comprehensive account of the Christian Socialist approach to all the problems of the day. It is felt, however, that they are worth publishing as a contribution to the discussion of some of these problems, and as an indication of the substantial measure of agreement that has been achieved between Christian Socialists of various points of view'.[29]

❑ **Since 1960**

Since the final formation of the Christian Socialist Movement there have been several key themes in Christian Socialism, namely: Liberation theology with its several offshoots; the Peace Movement; single issue campaigns; and the affiliation of the Christian Socialist Movement to the Labour Party in 1988.

Liberation theology

In 1972 the Peruvian priest Gustavo Guttierez published his *Theology of Liberation* in response to a series of discussions and experiences already vibrant, particularly within the Roman Catholic Church in Latin America. 'Theological reflection', it starts, '... the intelligence of faith, arises spontaneously and ineluctably within the believer, within all those who have received the gift of the word of God'.[30] The theological and political context was significant. For Vatican II had allowed Roman Catholics the opportunity to read the Bible in their own language, and in part Liberation theology represented a rediscovery of the biblical themes of exodus, jubilee, liberation within a sharply divided society where the majority were, in every definition of the term, poor. Dictatorship, neo-colonialism and a growing gap between rich and poor added strength to an analysis of faith that stressed above all the importance of the context of theology. A rich man talking about wealth and God would inevitably not come to the same conclusions as a poor woman, and it was the role of the Church to speak from the underbelly of society, from the vantage of the poor and the marginalised, rather than to prop up the ideological systems of capitalism and Coca-Cola imperialism. Just as God in the biblical record had a preferential option for the poor, so also the church.

Furthermore Guttierez, and many others such as Leonardo and Clodovis Boff, Jon Sobrino and Juan Luis Segundo, argued that the interpretation of the Bible should not be set purely in an academic circle, but in the context of action. It was not ortho-doxy but ortho-praxis that matters. The Basic Ecclesial Communities that arose throughout Latin America responded to this understanding of reading the Bible within a small group, within the poor community, and acting upon it. Theological reflection is then a secondary activity that responds to life, which in turn is to be transformed by reflection and action. Poverty itself, or a profound personal commitment to justice, are the preconditions of true Christian theology. Two successive conferences of Latin American bishops, at Puebla and Medellin, gave broad backing to both the theological methods of Liberation theology, and the need for the Church to adopt a preferential option for the poor.

Such Liberation theology has also become particularly significant within the churches of Africa and Asia. South Africa, where apartheid had politicised much of the church for many years, put a special emphasis on the concept of the 'kairos', the moment of judgement, that is not a delayed judgment at the end of time, but the moment now when, in Bible terms, God places before the people life and death that they may choose. Bishops such as Trevor Huddleston and Desmond Tutu, as well as Canon John Collins, Alan Boesak and others argue both that 'politics and faith are a seamless garment', and that apartheid offended against the very concept of God, for it denied that all were made equal and it used a supposedly religious principle to enforce oppression. The attempt in Britain to forge a Liberation Theology has primarily been represented by the work of the Urban Theology Unit at Sheffield under John Vincent, although the Bishop of Liverpool's book *Option for the Poor* made attempts at something similar. The enduring problem remains of whether people from a rich nation can argue a theology from poverty.

Other liberation theologies have also been particularly strong in the Western nations. Thus feminist theology, reasserting and discovering female images of God and enabling women to find a new emancipated role within the Church and society, has taken great strides in both America and Britain, and there is an incipient theology of gay and lesbian liberation being developed by such organisations as the Lesbian and Gay Christian Movement.

The Peace Movement

The concern for peace has always been a part of the radical Christian agenda, but the experience of two world wars, the invention and proliferation of nuclear weapons and the horrors of much modern warfare gave a special force to that concern from the 1960s through to today. Thus Donald Soper, the first Chair of the Christian Socialist Movement and its current President, has always described himself as a pacifist and would follow in the tradition of Keir Hardie and George Lansbury who opposed the First World War. And here the contribution of Christians to the left is most significant. Bruce Kent, Canon Collins, Christian CND and Pax Christi have all stood for a clear rejection of violence, using many of the non-violent campaigning methods of Martin Luther King and Gandhi.

Single Issue campaigns

When William Temple resigned from the Labour Party on becoming Bishop of Manchester, he signalled to many Christians that while it was appropriate for them to be involved in politics, it was not right to be involved in party politics. The major contribution that many radical Christians have therefore made to British society has been through campaigns on single issues, whether through the aid and development movement, the housing lobby or any of the health and education centred charities. It is vital then to recognise that the influence of radical Christian ideas and work is undoubtedly more extensive than any one movement. Britain's charitable system and voluntary organisations are the envy of Europe, and a cursory look just at the many organisations involved in Third World development will see the influence of both Liberation theology and Christian Socialist ideals of justice, equality, cooperation and peace.

In the 1980s, however, added strength was given by the work of organisations like Church Action on Poverty, the Churches National Housing Coalition and Catholic Housing Aid Society, as well as the Church Urban Fund which followed the publication of *Faith in the City*. Many Christian Socialists were involved in Amnesty International and the human rights movement, as well as the environmental campaigns.

Affiliation to the Labour Party

The years of Thatcherism, however, especially after a third General Election victory in 1988, made many Christians acknowledge that the politics of single issues rarely delivered change onto the Statute Book. Real change could only come about with a change of government. Yet many would not wish to relinquish heartfelt convictions for the simple sake of electability. Party politics is essentially a process of developing consensus, of compromise, and the hard rock of Christian radical idealism would seem to conflict with this.

But in 1988 the Christian Socialist Movement affiliated to the Labour Party as one of its Socialist Societies and decided that a vital part of its new role must be to act as a channel from the radical stream of Christian Socialism into the mainstream of national Party politics.

THE GRACE OF ALLIANCE

By 1993 this move had meant that a large number of Labour MPs had joined the Movement, as well as prominent members of the Shadow Cabinet. In 1993 the new Labour Leader, John Smith, addressed the movement's annual Tawney lecture, which was later published with others under the title *Reclaiming the Ground*. Drawing heavily on William Temple and Tawney he reasserted the fundamental issue as he then saw it: 'We should never underestimate the desire, which I believe is growing in our society, for a politics based on principle'.[31] The task of Christian Socialism has then been the delineation of what those principles might be, in the full recognition that others will have principles as well as Christians.

Another contributor to *Reclaiming the Ground*, Smith's successor as Labour Leader, Tony Blair, argues forcefully for the key principles of equality, 'not that we are uniform in character or position, but on the contrary that despite our differences we are entitled to be treated equally, without regard to our wealth, race, gender or standing in society', and does so from the same understanding of our basic humanity which is communal.[32]

Present day Christian Socialism is not, however, solely channelled through either the Christian Socialist Movement or through the Labour Party. The work of many other agencies and individuals stems equally from the radical Christian tradition.

Nonetheless, as Britain tries to reinterpret the Welfare State, as it reassesses its understanding of community and worries about criminality and develops a new philosophy of work, the possibility of radical change through a new government has become a determined aim for all on the Christian Left. The core ideas remain the same as for the early church, namely:

1. Property is not ultimately to be owned privately, but is held in trust for the common good.
2. As all humanity is made in the image of God, all are equal and to be treated with equal respect and to enjoy equal opportunities and access to education, health, employment and the fulfilment of their hopes and their potential.
3. As Christ became flesh so all human life is valuable, and the material concerns of human living are not to be dismissed.
4. As God made a preferential option for the poor it is incumbent upon Christians that they should seek to create a society where poverty is eradicated, and where poverty exists that the poor

are given shelter, food, drink, as of right. In particular justice must be equally accessible to the poor as to the rich, and a sharp divide between rich and poor cannot be just.
5. As God created humanity but gave us freedom to choose, social change and personal change must go hand in hand.
6. As Christ is described as The Prince of Peace, all who follow him are called to be peacemakers.

The radical agenda in Christian Socialism is clearly very traditional, based on the hard rock of a specifically theological mindset, but the history has been extremely varied, and has brought together many people who above all were of an independent spirit. Undoubtedly the future contribution of Christian Socialists will be equally eclectic.

God's programme to liberate the people is a transcendent one. Perhaps I repeat this idea too much, but I will keep on saying it. In wanting to solve immediate problems, we run the great danger of forgetting that immediate solutions can be mere sticking plasters and not real solutions. A genuine solution must fit into God's programme. Whatever solution we may decide on for a better land distribution, a better financial system for the country, a political arrangement better suited for the common good of the citizens, will have to be found in the context of definitive liberation.[33]

Chris Bryant is chair of the Christian Socialist Movement, and a Councillor in the London Borough of Hackney.

NOTES

1. Charles Gore *et al.*, *Property: its duties and rights* (Christain Social Union, 1913), pp. xiii–xiv.
2. St Cyprian, quoted in A Reid (ed.), *The New Party Described by Some of its Members*, p. 86.
3. John Chrysostom, *Homily 12 on 1 Timothy*, quoted in Clive Barrett, *To the Fathers they shall go* (Jubilee Group, 1984).
4. St Ambrose, quoted in Charles S Marson, *God's Co-operative Society* (1914), p. 95.
5. St Ambrose De Officiis Ministerium, 1:35, quoted in C Barrett *To the Fathers*, p. 35.
6. Ibid., 1:29, quoted ibid., p. 34.
7. R H Tawney, *Religion and the Rise of Capitalism* (Penguin, reprinted 1990).
8. Ibid., p. 176.

9. Gerard Winstanley, in Christopher Hill, *Winstanley: 'The Law of Freedom' and other Writings* (Cambridge University Press, 1973).
10. Ibid.
11. Ibid., 'New Years Gift', p. 204.
12. Karl Marx, *Capital*, vol. I (Everyman edition, 1948), p. 257.
13. George Stephens, in William Dale Morris, *The Christian Origins of Social Revolt* (Allen and Unwin, 1949), p. 170.
14. Frederick Dennison Maurice, *The Kingdom of Christ* (Macmillan, 1837).
15. G F Maurice, *Life of Frederick Dennison Maurice*, vol. II (Macmillan, 1884).
16. Maurice, letter to Kingsley, 2 January 1850.
17. Charles Kingsley, 'Letters to the Chartists', no. 2, quoted in *Politics for the People* (17 June 1948).
18. Steward Headlam, in *Christian Socialist* (February 1887).
19. *Rerum Novarum* (1891).
20. Cited in Peter d'A Jones, *The Christian Socialist Revival 1877–1914* (Princeton University Press, 1968), p. 241.
21. Ibid.
22. From *Industry and Property*, volume of Conference on Christian Politics, Economics and Citizenship *Reports*, 12 vols (Longman, 1924).
23. Ibid.
24. William Temple, in John Kent, *William Temple* (Cambridge University Press, 1992), pp. 155 and 158.
25. Ibid.
26. Ibid.
27. William Temple, *Christianity and Social Order* (Penguin, 1942).
28. R H Tawney, *Equality*, (Allen and Unwin, 1931), chapter 3.
29. *Papers from the Lamb* (Christian Socialist Movement, 1959).
30. Gustavo Guttierez, *Teologia de la Liberacion* (Ediciones Sigueme, 1972).
31. John Smith et al., in Christopher Bryant (ed.), *Reclaiming the Ground* (Spire, 1993).
32. Ibid.
33. Archbishop Oscar Romero on the day before his assassination, 24 March 1980 in *Romero, Martyr for Liberation* (CIIR, 1992), p. 12.

REVIEWS

NEW DIRECTIONS IN THE SOCIAL HISTORY OF NAZI GERMANY

David F Crew, ed., *Nazism and German Society 1933–1945*, (Routledge, London, 1994), 316 pp., ISBN 0 4150 8240 4, £11.99 paperback.

This book brings together nine major articles which have already appeared in Britain, Germany, Israel and the USA, and includes a useful original introduction by the editor. Together, the work is representative of some of the most important recent research on National Socialism, and the appearance of pieces which have until recently only been available in the German language is particularly to be welcomed.

As in any collection, the quality of the contributions is highly variable and it will be impossible to give them all equal treatment in the space of a short review. As Crew states, the value of the essays overall is that they 'draw attention to the multilayered, contradictory and complex realities of life in the Third Reich'.

All the articles summarise the main conclusions from the authors' previous work. Thus Omer Bartov's 'The Missing Years: German Workers, German Soldiers' is based on his book *Hitler's Army*. Alf Luedtke's important article 'The Honour of Labour: industrial workers and the power of symbols under National Socialism' was first published in K Tenfelde's collection *Arbeiter in 20 Jahrhunder*. Luedtke suggests that it was, among other things, the Nazis' attempts to exploit such themes as 'the honour of labour' and 'German quality work' that might explain the sympathy towards the Third Reich of some sections of the working class. Klaus N Mallmann and Gerhard Paul's article 'Omniscient, Omnipotent, Omnipresent? Gestapo, Society and Resistance' brings together the main conclusions from these German researchers' major 1991 study *Herrschaft und Alltag*. Based on a detailed social and political history of the Saar region under Nazism, Mallmann and Paul explain the methods which the Gestapo employed to establish support in Saar society, and look at how considerable sections of the working class were indispensable cogs in the machinery of persecution, exercising influence on developments through voluntary acts of denunciation of their neighbours and colleagues on a massive scale.

Other articles in the book concern women in the Third Reich (Gisela Bock and Adelheid von Salhern); the 'Hitler Myth' (Ian Kershaw summarises his well known but important conclusions); and the use of foreign labour in the war (Ulrich Albert's 70 page analysis of this takes up almost a quarter of the book!). The final piece is Christopher Brownin's 14 page 'One Day in Jozefow: initiation to mass murder'.

The most stimulating of the collection's articles, by Detlev Peukert on 'The Genesis of the Final Solution', has appeared twice previously – in his 1989 book *Max Weber Diagnise der Moderne,* and in the Childers and Caplan collection *Re-evaluating the Third Reich.* But it is a brilliant piece, tracing the origins of the 'Final Solution' in nineteenth-century 'scientific' ideologies. Peukert rejects the traditional explanation of the Holocaust's origins in antisemitism, adding an important dimension to the lively debate on the way in which the Third Reich expressed and shaped modern experience. It is unfortunate that there was not room in this collection to complement Peukert's arguments with contributions from Goetz Aly and Susanne Heim, who have stressed the importance of technocratic impulses in pointing a 'rational' way to the death camps.

Though the introduction and articles assembled in this book provide a good introduction to some of the most important aspects of social life under the Nazi regime, one discerns a list of absences: religion and religious mentalities; minority experiences, such as those of Jews and Gypsies; soldiers' lives in the barracks and at the front; social aspects of the Widerstand (resistance); and the social experience of the last year of the war, the way in which the reality of defeat was understood and lived in the months before the final capitulation of the regime. This might have been particularly interesting given the current focus on the 50th anniversary of the liberation. But one cannot have everything, and altogether this is a useful collection which makes the most important research findings of contemporary historians of the Third Reich available to students and general readers at a very reasonable price.

Oded Heilbronner

Oded Heilbronner works at The Centre of German History, The Hebrew University of Jerusalem.

John Saville, *The Politics of Continuity: British Foreign Policy and the Labour Government 1945–46*. (Verso, London and New York, 1993), ISBN 0 86091 456 9.

John Saville offers a series of explorations around a general theme, the early foreign policy of the postwar Labour Government. He begins with an extensive dissection of 'The Mind of the Foreign Office'; there then follows analyses of the politics of Ernest Bevin and Clement Attlee, with the latter emerging as a relative iconoclast on Middle Eastern Policy. The links between economic constraints and foreign policy are assessed; finally, there is a case study of Britain's intervention late in 1945 to restore French Colonial rule in Vietnam. Five appendices explore related episodes including an assessment of the relationship between the Labour Party's International Department especially its Secretary, Denis Healey, and Foreign Office officials. This provides the essential context to the production of *Cards on the Table*, the pro-Bevin 1947 Party document.

One major achievement is to illuminate important issues which have been ignored or marginalised by previous writers, most strikingly the British collaboration with the Japanese to suppress nationalist forces in Vietnam. The study rests firmly on the examination of government records and other private collections backed by a wealth of secondary materials. Together with Peter Weiler's excellent *British Labour and the Cold War* published in 1988, Saville's work makes a major contribution to a radical revisionist historiography of this important moment. Indeed some kind of revisionism is likely to become the new wisdom. As Saville notes, older 'respectable' views about the aggressive character of postwar Soviet policy have largely been rejected, not least by some former advocates. Thus Denis Healey looking back from the vantage point of 1989 commented, 'I think we were all mistaken'. This text makes an essential contribution from the Left to a necessary process of reassessment.

At one level its significance lies in its massively thorough demonstration of the character of British foreign policy. Foreign Office officials and most politicians assumed the desirability and the feasibility of Great Power status, and the durability of Empire. The latter depended on an almost complete myopia, with the exception of India, concerning the growth of powerful nationalist movements. Decision makers, including for the most part Labour Ministers, inhabited a house of illusions which protected a single-minded commitment to the restoration wherever possible of European colonialism.

One legacy of the analysis is to demonstrate that the election of a Labour Government was irrelevant to the direction of foreign policy. Contrary to some subsequent myths here was no progressive Administration gradually, and perhaps reluctantly, acknowledging the sombre evidence of Soviet intransigence and aggression. Rather the key figures, especially Bevin, simply acted on established assumptions about Britain's international role and the appropriate strategies for its protection. It was indeed 'the Politics of Continuity'.

This characterisation raises two broader and related issues; it is a strength of this book that the case studies are presented so as to encourage wider debate. First is the counterfactual – 'Could it have been otherwise?'. The other places this moment within the wider context of British decline. Assessment of the counterfactual requires a critical appraisal of the character of the Labour Party and the limits to its radical claims. Saville notes (p. 117) the existence of a significant alternative left tradition on international issues, partly Socialist but more often Radical Liberal. From the war in South Africa to the Civil War in Spain, a significant section of left opinion opposed the agendas and prejudices of the Establishment. Such sentiments left their mark on the interwar Labour Party and to some degree on the first two Labour Governments. In 1924, the Foreign Secretaryship was taken by MacDonald, a critic of British intervention in 1914; in 1929–31, the Government's foreign policy offered some limited compensation for party activists as the Government floundered in the face of economic crisis. Neither government offered a radical break with the past on international affairs but in both style and substance there seemed for many, sufficient to keep alive the idea of a distinctively Labour – perhaps Socialist – foreign policy. But in 1945, the change from Eden to Bevin was hardly noticeable.

The contrast can be exaggerated. Labour's international policy between the wars never questioned Britain's Great Power status. There was little scepticism about the desirability of Empire; indeed the Colonial policies of the first two Labour Governments were often thoroughly conservative. The dissenting tradition on international affairs was often a moralistic variant on the dominant establishment view. The propriety of Britain's international status was largely unquestioned; debate was often restricted to method. Yet granted the limitations of this tradition, it contrasted stylistically and to some extent substantively with the politics of Ernest Bevin. He was in some ways an archetypal labour movement product, but his experience specifically of the Labour Party and of its culture was limited. From 1910 to 1940 his preoccupations were industrial. His political interventions were often aggressive pronouncements on trade union priorities directed to career politicians whom he saw as slippery and multi-faced. One objective in such incursions was the exorcism of what he characterised as intellectual sentimentalities. Thus on foreign affairs the principle dissenting strand was not simply less radical than its rhetoric might suggest; it contested with a self-consciously realist view of power that reflected the ground rules of trade union negotiations. This latter perspective was often linked to an uncomplicated nationalism.

Saville is correct to emphasise that the government's foreign policy generated considerable criticism within the party during the first two years. The diverse strands within the more radical tradition were apparent in the Commons debate of November 1946 and in the conference debates of 1946 and 1947. Yet the leadership was never in serious danger of defeat. In part this security reflected broad support for the Government's domestic performance backed by a willingness to give the first majority Labour Government a fair chance. But it rested also on a strong trade union backing for the Administration. This was articulated by many Trade Union MPs and also by unions within the Party Conference. Saville refers to the protection of the Government by union block votes, but it would be useful to look further into this pattern of politics.

These were the years when the party leadership was reinforced by the alliance of the Transport Workers, the Miners and the General and Municipal Workers. Leading officials articulated the same political priorities as Bevin and rejected what they saw as the irresponsibility and naivete of alternative Party traditions. The leading officials of the Transport Workers and the Miners made their case with an abrasiveness that sometimes verged on authoritarianism. The internal factionalism of these unions, the battle between a majority Right and a minority Left harmonised neatly with the developing polarity of the Cold War. Within the General and Municipal Workers, Left politics was virtually absent; support for Bevin came in tones of measured moderation, a matter of clear 'common sense'. Although the Labour Party saw significant contests down to mid-1947 over international policy, the adversaries were unequal. If Labour Ministers would only break with the 'Politics of Continuity' through pressure within their party. Yet this was not a plausible alternative.

The politics of the Labour Party require location within the context of wider developments. The movement is one episode in a much larger chronicle not just of continuity, but of decline. Saville's diagnosis makes clear that Britain's political and administrative elites had their own distinctive arrogance and inadequacies. In part his explanation rests on the character of administrative personnel, the limited basis for recruitment to the Foreign Office, the bizarre smug assumptions of this closed world. Equally attention is paid (in Chapter 4) to the weaknesses within the British economy and the way in which early industrialisation spawned obsolescence. Moreover this problem was intensified by the conservatism and parochialism of political, administrative and educational elites with their indifference to any modernisation agenda. Whilst much of the 'Political Continuity' can be explained in the context of 'British Peculiarities', this moment must be situated within its global context. What options were feasible given the alignments and resource distributions of 1945? The detailed chapters offer routes into these fundamental debates.

Beyond the analysis of constraints and continuities, there is the question of creativity. Why were alternative views so scarce? Why had the Left so little to offer against the complacent established assumptions? The problem remains. After all, these ruins are inhabited.

David Howell

David Howell is Professor in the Department of Government, University of Manchester.

Lin Chun, *The British New Left* (Edinburgh University Press, Edinburgh, 1993), ISBN 0 7486 04227, £30 hardback.

After so many years, publication of the first full length study of the British New Left must be greeted with expectation. Leaving aside the various one-off pieces touching on the subject, Chun's study might be set alongside three collections of articles; David Widgery's *The Left in Britain*, the account of 1956 in the *Socialist Register* 1976, and the Oxford University's Socialist Discussion Group's *Out of Apathy*, and the booklength interview with Raymond Williams entitled 'Politics and Letters'. Though only the aptly named *Out of Apathy* was exclusively devoted to the New Left, it would not be unfair to view a first full study in the light of these previous accounts.

Lin Chun makes clear from the start that she is not a member of this 'British New Left'. Indeed Chun claims that she only became 'attracted by the New Left movement in Britain during the first year of [her] stay at Cambridge', while she had been 'working on a very different project' (p. xii). Given the degree of wrangling over the years among members of the British New Left, such deliberate distancing might be somewhat reassuring.

In a manner reminiscent of Stuart Hall, *The British New Left* firmly locates its starting point as the 'conjuncture' that was 1956 (Hall 1985, 1989). Divided into four partly chronological chapters, the book identifies its subject as a number of 'individual and collective activities associated with certain key publishing and research enterprises which formed the bases or organs of the movement' (p. xiii). An insight into these is offered in the contents page which cites a number of works which have become academic signposts. Proceeding book-by-book Chun provides an excellent review of the ideas about culture, historiography, class, revolution etc., that have characterised part of the intellectual Left over recent decades. The difficulty is whether it is reasonable to say that this history really represents something 'New'.

The first section; 'The Making of the New Left', charts briefly the historical details of 1956, the 'Middle Class Radicalism' (Parkin 1968) of CND and the establishing of the *Reasoner* and the *New Reasoner*, *Universities* and *Left Review*, and the infamous merger that produced *New Left Review*. It must be said here that the impressive array of interviews completed by Chun has been put to good use in describing the activities of a number of persons at this time. What is perhaps less apparent are the various emotions that these difficult years invoked, and which necessarily played a crucial part in the future of the Left.

The next two chapters are largely devoted to the publications cited in the contents pages. Each is given a section in which they are thoughtfully reviewed. Reading through these I was reminded of the arguments carried through in History Workshop and *New Left Review* in the later 1970s. The distinct advantage here though was that the artificial divides between say the 'historical' and the 'literary' etc. are overcome so that it became easier to get an overall picture of the main contours against which individual arguments were set. The fourth and last chapter continues the themes of the previous two, bringing us forward to the ideas of 'Western Marxism', 'cultural materialism', and 'methodology and historiography'.

The chapter ends with a discussion of the rediscovery of feminist theory for which Chun argues the New Left were in part responsible. Unfortunately, reflecting the contents elsewhere in the book, the connection cited is taken from an (incorrect) intellectual history, rather than any wider social and political development. Finally a short epilogue traces the metamorphosis of the New Left in the form of 'the New Social Movements'.

It is perhaps the bringing together of so many different topics that should be seen as the primary achievement of the the British New Left. Indeed as a history of ideas Chun has provided a highly readable account of what have at times been writings where theoretical abstraction seems to have been given priority over clarity of communication. On that account alone *The British New Left* deserves to be widely read. But even more necessary than this is arguably the clarifying of the political project of the 'New Left'. On this score Chun's account has the unfortunate tendency at times to read like a very good account of the conditions for the rise of certain new academic fields of study.

❏ An alternative history

To best appreciate Chun's account of the New Left I want to proceed by placing alongside it an alternative history. This is in part taken from those accounts referred to earlier, though the manner of its linking is my own. The first section of Chun's study is, as I said earlier, an account of the rise of the New Left '... the origins of the New Left in Britain were ... highly specific. It came into being in 1956–57 under the double shock of the Hungarian uprising and the Suez Crisis, which had shaken the political configuration of the British left'(p. 1). Chun continues: 'The Twentieth Congress of the Communist Party of the Soviet Union (CPSU), to which Khrushchev gave his secret speech concerning the truth about Stalin, was the watershed' (p. 1).

One might wish for a little less generalisation about 'the British left' but as a citing of what were undoubtedly significant political events the point is hard to quarrel with. The more important point about these lines though is their capturing of what is the real historical problem of *The British New Left*.

It is arguably the prerogative of each generation to write history from its own position. Indeed it might be argued by some at least there is no other way history can be written. Certainly to identify 1956 as a break with the past and the start of something new, provides an opportunity to construct a narrative in which certain activities and figures gain centre stage for the constructing of political identities. There can be little doubt that for *The British New Left* these were selected editors of *New Left Review* in the 1960s and 1970s. Such centring is certainly necessary if any of us are to have a sense of place. The danger I want to point to here is when a 'break' becomes so emphasised that the very real continuities with past political formations are obscured.

It must be said immediately that Chun does not avoid this difficult issue. In a section entitled 'some notes on definitions' (pp. 16–19), Chun differentiates the New Left from that which it was not. This other, 'the whole traditional left', includes 'Communists, Trotskyists, trade unions militants, the Fabians and radical intellectuals' (p. 16). Chun argues that when these 'main received political traditions of the left had irretrievably broken down; then a New Left came into being' (p. 17). The effect of such defining can only reinforce the idea of break and difference.

There are perhaps two points to be made here. One, which I will only cite and move on, is the minimal space given in this the key chapter of Chun's book to the more general political developments from Suez to the 1959 General Election. The same goes for the debates across the Left epitomised by Hugh Gaitskill's pledge to 'Fight fight and fight again to save the Labour Party we love'.

❏ The libertarian tradition

The second point though is to question whether the libertarian values which the 'New Left' so vigorously proclaimed, can be separated from so much that had gone before. There is not the space here to develop the point fully and I will cite only three examples suggesting in different ways a strong continuity with the past. The first refers to the *Reasoner*. Edited by two members of the CP historians' group, the internal party publication, far from starting some thing 'new', would seem to have been trying to reclaim a tradition of radicalism and internationalism stifled by Party fears and a seeming deadening bureaucracy. The tradition of Communists with which Thompson and Saville identified evolved from the Popular Front, Spain, the Partisan movement, and the 'Railway Adventure' in Yugoslavia.

Coinciding with the start of this period was the publication of A L Morton's *A People's History of England*. Under the watchful eye of the all too little remembered Donna Torr, this creation of a radical lineage was furthered by what in any terms was the magnificent achievement of the building of a new history in which the tracing out of the resistance to the 'Norman Yoke' was carried on. Set against these experiences and intellectual activity, the *Reasoner* could be interpreted as an attempt to continue a project which might otherwise be lost under what appeared to be a canopy of lies, denial and deceit. As John Saville put it (Socialist Register 1976):

> ... we were of one mind in our insistence that if the British CP was to recover its self respect, let alone the respect of the labour movement in general, it must encourage an honesty of discussion that would undoubtedly, be painful to many. ... we had agreed first that the Party leadership was deliberately curbing and confining discussion, and second that the most obvious way to force an open debate was probably to publish independently of the Party press.

The second point is taken from an account of the time from an ex-Secretary of the Partisan Club in London. In it Ioan Davies suggests that far from being a new formation the New Left simply lived in 'the animated presence of existing bodies of labouring intellectuals plus a few middle-class intellectuals who saw the meaning of their work as having presence in the life-blood of those whose ideas were generated by their everyday experience' (Ioan Davies 1993 pp. 118–119).

❏ New? Left

Arguably the most important grouping here was the WEA which elsewhere Raymond Williams has cited as a key formation for the development of a distinct political project (Williams 1989). There has unfortunately been no published study as yet of the role of the WEA in the left of the later 1950s, though Fieldhouse's work on a slightly earlier period may be informative (Fieldhouse 1985). What is certain is that many of the people engaged in the 'New Left' came from Adult Education backgrounds.

Bringing together the questions of experience and intellectual lineage on the one hand, and the actual composition of the New Left on the other, it might be asked what the term 'New' Left actually refers to. Put another way, the question is perhaps why the term 'New

Left' has been able to become so established? In answering this we can recognise an element of self-invention here. Some academics write some books, which other academics group together, in this case under the heading 'the New Left', which is then rightly defined as a collection of intellectual activities.

What I have suggested here is that it might be justified to rethink '1956', to move away from it being a break for which a suitable label is coopted, to refer to a reaffirmation of a non-aligned radical libertarian tradition, and a linking up again with older causes which the pressures of the Cold War had forced into quiescence. Were this done then it may be possible to fit the New Left into a longer history, a project of a particular form of politics. Indeed, and this is my third example, just such a continuation is alluded to by Raymond Williams in a typically cryptic comment in an interview with *New Left Review* in 1979:

> I still believe that the failure to fund the working class movement culturally when the channels of popular education and popular culture were there in the forties became a key factor in the very quick disintegration of Labours position in the fifties. I don't think that you can understand the projects of the New Left in the late fifties unless you realize that people like Edward Thompson and myself ... were positing the recreation of that kind of union.

The point links up with that made earlier about adult education and the other networks through which the actual existence of the New Left is to be found.

❑ Theoreticism

But the rearranging rests finally on two important conclusions. The first concerns the manner in which a history is interpreted. In the case of the New Left the tendency has been to emphasise theoretical and conceptual issues at the expense of any real political context. What then happens is that these 'texts' are analysed for their theoretical adequacy rather than for any adequacy as responses to felt political forces. On this score we might note how, for instance, Raymond Williams can appear on the reading lists of Cultural Studies degrees but remain completely unknown to a student of Politics.

The second conclusion refers to the manner in which a generation may think itself to be facing something entirely new. In consequence it spends a great deal of time thinking through a suitably new response.

Of course circumstances change, but that does not mean to say that nothing can be learnt from the efforts of others who have gone before us. Rethinking the New Left in terms of a continued attempt to link a popular educational project with a wider political movement might to that end be extremely useful. Chun's identifying of 'key publishing and research enterprises' is on that account absolutely right, though the absence of Merlin Press from the index might seem a little surprising. What is less certain is whether *The British New Left* really is a study of such efforts. Admittedly it would be much more difficult than any history of ideas, but what we need is a little more emphasis on the actual attempts to carry through those projects and a little less on the conceptual, academic, ideas which the experience of those projects produced.

Did someone say 'historical materialism'?

Stephen Woodhams

Stephen Woodhams works in the faculty of Health Care and Social Studies of the University of Luton.

❑ Bibliography

Ioan Davies, 'Cultural Theory in Britain', *Theory, Culture and Society* vol. 10, 1993.

Peggy Duff, *Left, Left, Left* (Alison and Busby, 1971).

Roger Fieldhouse, *Adult Education and the Cold War* (University of Leeds, 1985).

Stuart Hall, 'The New Left 1956–1968' London History Workshop, 10 September 1985, unpublished.

———, 'The "First" New Left: Life and Times', *Out of Apathy* (Verso, 1989).

Frank Parkin, *Middle-Class Radicalism* (Manchester University Press, 1968).

Socialist Register (Merlin, 1976).

David Widgery, *The Left in Britain 1956–1968* (Peregrine Books, 1976).

Raymond Williams, *What I Came to Say* (Hutchinson, 1989).

———, *Politics and Letters* (New Left Books, 1979).

Stephen Woodhams, 'Writing culture and politics in the cold war', *Socialist History* issue 5, 1994.

MUGGLETONIAN MARXISM

E P Thompson, *Witness Against the Beast: William Blake and the Moral Law* (Cambridge University Press, Cambridge, 1993), xxi and 234pp., ISBN 0 521 22515 9, £17.95.

One could not know much of E P Thompson without realising that he was haunted in later life by problems, which he felt to be somehow related, concerning the poet Blake, and the flagging vitality of the labour movement in Britain. He was looking back (but also forward, as his crusade against nuclear armaments showed) for light on the one, and a rekindling for the other. He looked back to his own earlier years, and much further back, to the early times of a people's struggle for emancipation. This book, completed not long before his death, is an exploration of Blake's thinking, especially of its remoter sources. Many of its readers will have been expecting an investigation of social and political influences; but as he explains at the outset, he believed that this had been sufficiently done by others, particularly by his friend David Erdman. What had not been made enough of was Blake's very individual interpretation of Christianity. This is summed up in the term 'Antinomianism'. Thompson was a good deal of an antinomian himself, of a different genus; he was convinced of 'the ubiquity and centrality of antinomian tenets to Blake's thinking' (p. 18).

They helped, no doubt, to make him a permanent oppositionist, a man always, like the Irishman, 'agin the government'. But what other benefit could be derived, at a date when modern industrialism was getting into its stride, from the tortuous complexities of whether, or how far, or in what sense, the Mosaic code of morality was cancelled by Christ's sacrifice, is far less easy to see; and Thompson cannot be said to make clear enough its significance either for Blake or for himself. In England the extreme antinomian position came to the front in the mushrooming of disoriented sects about 1650, after Cromwell imposed his ban on any further political progress or social change. Ranter, Quaker, and similar ideas and practices, often freakish, were a consolation, a substitute for the real enfranchisement that England was being baulked of. No amount of Ranting and raving could make up for political defeat. When Thompson affirms that 'The closer we are to 1650, the closer seem to be to Blake' (p. 46), he risks reminding us not of Blake the true prophet, but of the poet in his long twilight, living among shades of things long since grown meaningless, and talking endlessly to himself.

What Thompson needed, or convinced himself that he needed, was firm evidence – not discovered by Hill or Morton – of historical links, a continuity of ideas, between the sectaries of 1650 and Blake. It could only be through some hidden channel, like an underground tunnel in Persia carrying irrigation water to distant fields. Among the brood of sects some of which lingered on at least into the eighteenth century (though Quakerism, at any rate, greatly transformed), Thompson came to take a special interest in the one founded by Ludowick Muggleton, unchanged within but outwardly soon content with a troglodyte existence, seeking no converts and only jealously guarding its (in some ways grotesque) theological legacy. After many bafflements, our explorer found himself face-to-face with this legacy, stored in eighty packing-cases, and with its guardian, the last surviving Muggletonian. There is nothing to show that Blake was ever a member; he may well have been familiar with beliefs of the same kind.

Thompson contrasts this heterodox religious tradition with a very different one, sponsored by Katherine Raine and deriving from the far more distant regions of Porphyry and Plotinus and Neoplatonism: a theory 'academic to the core', and with none of Blake's 'radical edge and bite' (pp. xvi and xviii). But if Katherine Raine's study is one of bloodless over-intellectualism – he allows it some 'genuine insights and discoveries' (p. 210) – Thompson's alternative suffers from an opposite defect of anti-intellectualism. Sects like the Muggletonians were ready, quite unlike the broad mainstream of Dissent, to accept and make a virtue of exclusion from up-to-date education and thought. Blake himself regarded Reason, that idol of the Enlightenment, as 'the Satanic principle', entirely materialistic and mercenary (p. 94). Thompson qualifies this by observing that what radicals like Blake denounced would be renamed by Karl Marx as 'ideology', the 'compulsive restraints' imposed on men's minds by the warping interests of their rulers (p. 109). Blake would have performed a better service if he had worked this out for himself and spread it to others, instead of abandoning Hamlet's 'godlike reason' to the jackals of private property. It may be recalled that when Thompson was breaking with his party's bureaucracy, the name he and his associates gave to their journal was not the *Ranter*, but the *Reasoner*.

Two handfuls of short poems gave Blake his place among the great English poets: *Songs of Innocence* (1789) and *Songs of Experience*

(1795). They clearly owed very much to the enthusiastic hopes amid which this short span of years began, and the disappointment clouding its end. Yet it is characteristic of this poet that in the year when the French Revolution opened and the Bastille fell, he was joining a 'New Church' in London, a congregation (soon, like the leadership in Paris, at odds with itself) of followers of Swedenborg, the Swedish government official and scientist turned mystic. When disillusionment with the revolution came, and Wordsworth took refuge in Dove Cottage, Blake could find no better retreat than a cloudy inner world of his own. From the turmoil of 1650 there had been preserved 'a vocabulary of symbolism, a whole cluster of signs and images', and they reappear, reshuffled, in Blake's picture and his lengthy rhapsodic poems (p. 91; cf.115), which they made it impossible for anyone else to understand. Their most compulsive and least attractive symbol was the serpent; one must wonder why, or how many real snakes Blake had ever seen. Thompson sensibly makes no attempt to interest us in 'the impossible labours of the prophetic books', the endeavour to put together a 'syncretic mythology' (p. 215). Blake could no more turn his rusty counters into poetry than alchemy, even Isaac Newton's, could turn lead into gold. In his later years he was becoming 'wilful and somewhat cranky' (pp. 223–4).

It may seem now and then as if this protracted search for an answer to one of the Sphinx of History's riddles might have been left to a harmless antiquarian. Yet the book has many compensations to offer. Even on its more arid side it bears witness to the descent, too often forgotten by Marxists, of socialism from Christianity. Thompson was at home with the psychology of religion; this showed in his account of Methodism and the factory worker, and it shows again here, even in his comments on so recondite a doctrine as that of imputed righteousness (p. 162). His fine ear for poetry is evident all through a very detailed commentary on the poem 'London' (p. 174ff.).

Its author may have lost his inspiration, but unlike Wordsworth or Coleridge he never went over to the enemy, or sank into tame conformity; as Thompson says, he went on to the end calling himself a Son of Liberty and wearing publicly the red cap of the republic. As for the Muggletonian Church, after two centuries of invisibility it has received a generous funeral monument; a memorial which could have been raised by no one but Edward Thompson, the most exceptional among all the bevy of socialist historians he belonged to. And there

REVIEWS

are touches of wry humour in this record of long-drawn, and confessedly only in part successful, wanderings in the wilderness.

V G Kiernan

Victor Kiernan is Emeritus Professor of Modern History in the University of Edinburgh and has written extensively on historical themes.

Christopher Hill, *The English Bible and the Seventeenth Century Revolution* (Penguin Books, Harmondsworth, 1993), ISBN 0 14 014990 8, £8.99 paperback.

❏ **The Bible's ancestry**

It is most probable that speech, culture – and religion – all appeared together with the emergence of *homo sapiens* somewhere between 100,000 and 50,000 years ago.

Although great caution has to be exercised in drawing any conclusions about our remote forebears from the evidence of surviving hunter-gatherer communities in the twentieth century, it again appears to be highly probable that the original form of religion involved totemic relationships with the food animals and plants upon which such communities depended for survival. I have sometimes speculated whether the Garden of Eden myth, in which the primal sin and disobedience was centred on eating, might not preserve a folk-memory of a pre-agricultural past when subsistence did not have to be gained through perpetual and relentless toil. After all, the curse that was laid on Adam was to become an arable farmer.

At any rate, with the development of settled agriculture, then subsequently cities and states largely predatory upon surrounding agrarian populations, religion was predominantly a matter of civic or royal cults, which served the functions both of providing access to the supernatural world through its priestly functionaries and acting as mechanisms of social control and status signification.

Michael Mann in *The Sources of Social Power* has argued that the contradictions and antagonisms inherent in societies of such a kind lie at the source of what he terms the 'salvation religions', which all emerged in a period of roughly 2000 years, beginning with the Hindu religion/culture and ending with Islam. Certainly these were also community faiths, otherwise they could never have got off the ground, but what set them apart was firstly that they transcended the boundaries of the merely local cults which they displaced or evolved out of, and secondly that they placed their adherents as individuals in a personal relationship to the divine – one only has to read the Book of Job to appreciate how this applied in ancient Judaism.

The latter faith, following the Babylonian exile, was also distinguished in the ancient world by its monotheism, and owing to the peculiarities of its evolution, by an attention and regard for social justice and righteous government, sentiments which were embodied principally in its prophetic writings. (See the article by Chris Bryant in this issue).

Jesus of Nazareth was of course a Jewish prophet (and perhaps a revolutionary), at a time when the country lay under foreign occupation and the religion was itself splintered and in turmoil. The faith which was constructed around his name therefore had a Judaic foundation. However it was in many ways a syncretic amalgam, being also mixed with Greek philosophy and the mystery cults which flourished in the late Hellenistic world. These offered personal salvation, gained through secret knowledge, to their initiates.

A compound faith of this sort was tailor-made for the conditions of late antiquity and the declining Roman empire, as economic insecurity, state rapacity, civil conflict and barbarian invasion grew inexorably from generation to generation. Unlike the mystery cults it did not require a heavy admission fee. It held out to its adherents the promise of eternal life, together with a supportive community in the present one and above all a convincing explanation to the faithful of their place and destiny in the world and the world hereafter. Its growth proved unstoppable. In the end the authorities, on the principle that if you can't beat them, join them, made it the official religion.

Although increasingly ritualised from that point, Christianity remained nevertheless a religion of the book. It took over the Jewish scriptures, rearranging them to purportedly predict the birth of Christ, and to these it added a selection of narratives and epistles from its early decades. This collation is what we term the Christian Bible.

Arising out of the prophetic tradition the scriptures of Judaism and the two faiths descended from it, Christianity and Islam – in spite of manifold texts justifying subordination and acquiescence – nonetheless carry a revolutionary charge which hierarchical and oppressive regimes claiming to be based upon these religions have always found very difficult to handle. During the medieval ages one answer of the feudal church was to confine the scriptures to a language intelligible only to its own functionaries – yet even so, popular revolts erupted from century to century, claiming the justice and equality said to be proclaimed in the Old or New Testament.

The Reformation of the sixteenth century was a social and political, as well as a religious, revolution – one easily expropriated, like Christianity before it, by ruling classes and elites. In challenge to the authority of the pope and the priestly hierarchy it had set up the authority of the vernacular Bible, which the new-fangled technology of printing disseminated far and wide. Although it was interpreted in such a manner as to underpin the authority of the princes who backed the reformed faith, even at the beginning of the process perceptive observers realised that it would not remain so: 'Our holy prelates [say that God's word] causeth insurrection and teacheth the people to disobey ... and moveth them to rise against their princes, and to make all common and to make havoc of other men's good's'. Thus wrote William Tyndale, the biblical translator, in 1528.

❏ The Bible in the Revolution

The above quotation opens Christopher Hill's exploration of the years when for a brief and unique space of time the Bible supplied the ideological energy for revolutionary politics in a recognisably modern form, when the argument over monarchy, representative government or dictatorship was conducted with reference to ancient Israel and the apocalypse was linked with the reformation of parliament.

Christopher Hill is a historian who has himself been responsible for a seventeenth-century revolution by the introduction of Marxist perspectives to those decades of transformation. The years between 1640 and 1660 form one of the most disputed themes in British historical writing, and it is no exaggeration to say that all the worthwhile historical writing in this area during the past 35 years or so has been produced either in extension of, or in reaction to, the interpretations which he has advanced.

With his historiographical energy in no way diminished, Hill now opens up a further dimension of the revolutionary years; the centrality of the Bible to all the debates over forms of government and social reorganisation, its adoption as the manifesto of every party and faction, each of which could find in its diffuse and contradictory content whatever they needed to suit their political stances or social agendas.

The book is organised thematically rather than chronologically: the author defines it as being less a structured study and more a series of essays around a common theme. There are innumerable fascinating insights. It is well known for example that Charles I was stigmatised by his puritan enemies as 'the Man of Blood', for apparently obvious reasons. Hill notes that he himself had assumed as much until reading an article by Patricia Crawford which demonstrated that the actuality behind this phrase was less an indictment of the King as a war criminal than his identification with 'men of blood' referred to in the Bible, whose own blood must be shed to cleanse the land. A chapter is devoted to elaborating upon this point.

Another intriguing curiosity is the Geneva Bible, now forgotten by all but specialist historians, but in the sixteenth and seventeenth centuries of central significance. The translation was produced by English exiles in Geneva in the time of Queen Mary and was the first to divide chapters into verses, but its importance lay in the marginal notes with which it was supplied and which were, in the period of its ascendancy, treated with almost as much reverence as the scripture itself. Religiously radical though socially conservative, this commentary did much to prepare the ground for the puritan revolution.

In the end the English Bible was the victim of its revolutionary success, as Hill demonstrates in his chapter headed 'The Bible Dethroned'. Such use had been made of it by subversives and revolutionaries that in the restored royalist England after 1660 it could never recover its status as the presumed arbiter of social and political values, and before too long ceased to be quoted in serious political contexts. This was less true in Scotland, and much less true in the north of Ireland and what was to become the United States. The latter two societies continue to be haunted by the spectre of biblical politics and bigotry to a degree inconceivable anywhere else in the west. Reading this stimulating volume cannot fail to provoke reflection on the manner in which documents originating in utterly remote times and largely incomprehensible purposes can possess a reach extending to thousands of years after their composition.

Willie Thompson

BOOKS RECEIVED

Reviews of some of the following items are in preparation and will appear in future issues of the journal. Publishers are urged to send items to be considered for review to the editorial team, care of the address on the cover of the journal. Readers interested in reviewing items are also invited to contact the editorial team.

Max Adereth, *Line of March: an historical and critical analysis of British communism and its revolutionary strategy* (Praxis Press, London, 1994), 153pp. ISBN 1 8991 5500 7, £8.99 paperback.

Johann P Arnason, *The Future That Failed : origins and destinies of the Soviet Model*, (Routledge, London, 1994), xi and 239pp., ISBN 0 4150 6227 6, £12.99 paperback.

George J Barnsby, *History of Wolverhampton, Bilston and District Trades Union Council 1865–1990*, (Wolverhampton, Bilston and District Trades Union Council, Wolverhampton, 1994), 95pp., ISBN 0 9523 9600 9, £5.00 (£2.50 and 50p postage and packing to trade unionists).

Stefan Berger, *The British Labour Party and the German Social Democrats: a comparative study* (Clarendon Press, Oxford, 1994), xiii and 302pp., ISBN 0 1982 0500 7, hardback.

Martin Blinkhorn, *Mussolini and Fascist Italy* (second edition) (Routledge/Lancaster Pamphlets, London, 1994), xv and 64pp., ISBN 0 4151 0231 6, £4.99 paperback.

Joanna Bourke, *Working Class Cultures in Britain 1890–1960: gender, class and ethnicity* (Routledge, London, 1994), x and 275pp., ISBN 0 4150 9898 X, £12.99 paperback.

John Burnett, *Idle Hands: the experience of unemployment 1790–1990*, (Routledge, London, 1994), ix and 368pp., ISBN 0 4150 5501 6, £14.99 paperback.

R J Crampton, *Eastern Europe in the Twentieth Century* (Routledge, London, 1994), xx and 475pp., ISBN 0 4150 5346 3, £14.99 paperback.

David F Crew, ed., *Nazism and German Society 1933–1945* (Routledge, London, 1994), xi and 316pp., ISBN 0 4150 8240 4, £11.99 paperback.

Richard Crockatt, *The Fifty Years War: the United States and the Soviet Union in World Politics*, (Routledge, London, 1994), xviii and 417pp., ISBN 0 4151 0471 8, £25.00 hardback.

Radhika Desai, *Intellectuals and Socialism: 'Social Democrats' and the Labour Party* (Lawrence and Wishart, London, 1995), vi and 217pp., ISBN 0 8531 5795 2, £14.99 paperback.

Claire Duchen, *Women's Rights and Women's Lives in France 1944–1968*, (Routledge, London, 1994), xiii and 253pp., ISBN 0 4150 0934 0, £12.99 paperback.

John Eldridge and Lizzie Eldridge, *Raymond Williams: Making Connections* (Routledge, London, 1994), vii and 240pp., ISBN 0 4150 4088 4, £12.99 paperback.

Nicholas Ellison, *Egalitarian Thought and Labour Politics: retreating visions* (Routledge, London, 1994), xiv and 310pp., ISBN 0 4150 6972 6, £40.00 hardback.

Nina Fishman, *The British Communist Party and the Trade Unions 1933–1945*, (Scolar Press, Aldershot, 1995), xi and 380pp., ISBN 1 8592 8116 8, £45.00 hardback.

James Hinton, *Shop Floor Citizens: engineering democracy in 1940s Britain* (Edward Elgar Publishing, Cheltenham, 1994), viii and 222pp., ISBN 1 8589 8081 X, £39.95 hardback.

Jean Jones, *Ben Bradly: fighter for India's freedom: occasional papers series no 1* (Socialist History Society, London, 1994), 40pp., ISBN 0 9523 8100 1, £2.50 (£2.00 including postage and packing to members of Socialist History Society).

Melvyn Leffler and David Painter, eds, *Origins of the Cold War: an international history* (Routledge, London, 1994), xiii and 322pp., ISBN 0 4150 9694 4, £12.99 paperback.

Trevor Lumis, *The Labour Aristocracy 1851–1914* (Scolar Press, Aldershot, 1994), xii and 190pp., ISBN 1 8592 8049 8, £35.00 hardback.

Stepan G Mestrovic, *The Balkanization of the West; the confluence of postmodernism and postcommunism* (Routledge, London, 1994), xiv and 226pp., ISBN 0 4150 8755 4, £13.99 paperback.

Seumas Milne, *The Enemy Within: MI5, Maxwell and the Scargill Affair* (Verso, London, 1994), viii and 344pp., ISBN 0 8609 1461 5, £16.95 hardback.

John Newsinger, *Fenianism in Mid-Victorian Britain*, Socialist History of Britain Series, (Pluto Press, London, 1994), 102pp., ISBN 0 7453 0899 6, £6.95 paperback.

BOOKS RECEIVED

Bryan D Palmer, *E P Thompson: objections and oppositions* (Verso, London, 1994), xiii and 201pp., ISBN 1 8598 4970 1, £34.95, 1 8598 4070 1, £11.95 paperback.

Geoffrey Pridham and Tatu Vanhanen, eds, *Democratization in Eastern Europe: domestic and international perspectives* (Routledge, London, 1994), xiv and 274pp., ISBN 0 4151 1064 5, £12.99 paperback.

Raphael Samuel, *Theatres of Memory: past and present in contemporary culture* (Verso, London, 1995), xiii and 479pp., ISBN 0 8609 1209 4, £18.95 hardback.

Mike Savage and Andrew Miles, *The Remaking of the British Working Class 1840–1940* (Routledge, London, 1994), xi and 106pp., ISBN 0 4150 7320 0, £6.99 paperback.

John Saville, *The Consolidation of the Capitalist State 1800–1850*, Socialist History of Britain Series, (Pluto Press, London, 1994), 91pp., ISBN 0 7453 0897 X, £6.95 paperback.

Eric Shaw, *The Labour Party Since 1979: crisis and transformation* (Routledge, London, 1994), xvii and 261pp., ISBN 0 4150 5615 2, £13.99 paperback.

Mike Squires, with personal recollections by Noreen Branson, *The Aid To Spain Movement in Battersea 1936–1939* (Elmfield Publications, London, 1994), 64pp., ISBN 0 9524 0290, £4.50 paperback.

Ernie Trory, *How Did It Happen? The dialectics of counter-revolution* (Crabtree Press, Hove, 1994), 84pp., ISBN 0 9515 0984 5, £3.75 paperback.

John Wolffe, *God and Greater Britain: religion and national life in Britain and Ireland 1843–1945*, (Routledge, London, 1994), xi and 324pp., ISBN 0 4150 3570 8, £40.00 hardback.

JOIN THE SOCIALIST HISTORY SOCIETY

The Socialist History Society is the heir to a long tradition of Marxist historical study, associated with many eminent historians of the left and marked by regular publications, including over eighty monographs. The work of our members, past and present, has had a far-reaching effect on the perception and teaching of history.

Although the scope of the society is not confined to the recent past, we are especially concerned with labour and democratic history and with the history of women's and black movements. In particular we aim to contribute to an understanding of the history of socialist and revolutionary movements in the twentieth century, to understand both their failures and achievements.

The Society is registered with the Democratic Left but is open to everyone interested in its aims, irrespective of their political or other affiliations. Activities include regular historical discussions and meetings, assistance to researchers, and publications.

Members are entitled to participate in all the Society's activities and be elected to its committee and offices. Membership includes subscription to *Socialist History* without further payment, a very considerable saving.

Annual subscription for individuals is £15 waged, £10 unwaged, £20 institutions, £20 overseas members.

Send subscription with name and address to:

Secretary,
Socialist History Society,
6, Cynthia Street,
London N1 9JF

INDEX

Acland, Sir Richard 96
Adereth, Max 73
Allied Supreme War Council 19
Attlee, Clement Richard 10, 11, 106
Austria 10

Balkans, the 22
Baltic, the 19
Beaverbrook, Lord 56
Belgium 14
Bellers, John 88
Bevin, Ernest 28, 43, 49, 55, 60, 62, 106–8
Blair, Tony 79, 101
Blake, William 12, 88, 116–19
Britain 7, 8, 10, 11, 14–17, 19–25, 27, 28, 72, 86, 87, 89, 104, 106, 109, 116, 122
Bruce, David 23

Cadogan, Sir Alexander 15
Canada 20
Chamberlain, Neville 16, 20, 21, 22, 23, 35
Chrystostom, John 84
Churchill, Sir Winston 10, 17, 28, 72
Clark, Alan 19
Cobbett, William 89
Cold War, the 72, 108, 114
Communist Party 19, 27–9, 5–5, 61, 63, 64, 73, 76, 111–13
Conze, Dr Edward 13
Cromwell, Oliver 76, 86, 87, 116
Czechoslovakia 10, 22, 76

Davies, Joseph E 18
Davis, William Rhodes 21, 23
Deutscher, Isaac 73, 76
Disraeli, Benjamin 90
Dusseldorf accords, the 20, 24

Eden, Anthony 107

Elleinstein, Jean, 73
Emergency Order 43
Essential Works Order (EWO) 28, 32, 63

Finland 19, 20, 74
First World War 11, 14, 28–30, 41, 63–5, 94, 99
Fox, George 87
France 8, 14, 16, 17, 19, 20, 21, 92, 118

Gallacher, Willie 29, 43
Germany 7–9, 14–16, 18–19, 21–5, 75–6, 104–5
Goering, Hermann 24
Gore, Charles 83, 93
Gray, John 29, 31, 33, 34, 48–51, 53, 54, 56, 58, 61
Gromyko, Andrey Andreyevich 73, 76
Groves, Reg 13
Guttierez, Gustavo 98

Hardie, Keir 93, 94, 99
Headlam, Stewart Duckworth 92, 93
Henderson, Sir Neville 20
Hess, Rudolf 19
Hitler, Adolf 9, 10, 15, 16, 18, 19, 24, 72, 74, 75
Hobsbawm, Eric 8
Hughes, Thomas 91
Hungary 76, 111

Inskip, Sir Thomas 15
Italy 8, 16, 22

Japan 15, 22, 75, 106

Kennedy, Joseph P 21
Khrushchev, Nikita 76, 111
Kingsley, Charles, 90, 91, 92

Labour Party 6, 10, 11, 29, 61, 72, 93–5, 97, 98, 100, 101, 106–9
Lansbury, George 94, 95, 99
Laud, William 86
Laws, Margaret 15
Lenin, Vladimir Ilyich Ulyanov 8, 14, 74, 77
Litvinov, Maxim 18
Londonderry, Lord 24

Maclean, Fitzroy 18
Maloney, A 48
Malthus, Thomas Robert 90
Marx, Karl Heinrich 13, 88
Maurice, Frederick Dennison 90, 91, 92
Mayhew, Henry 91
McShane, Harry 64
Medvedev, Roy 73
Middle East 22, 25, 106
Molotov, Vyacheslav Mikhaylovich 18, 24, 75
Molotov-Ribbentrop pact, the 18, 24
More, Hannah 89
Morgan, Dave 11
Munich 20, 21, 22
Munzer, Thomas 85
Mussolini, Benito 15

Nazis 9, 11, 18, 20, 21, 24, 74, 104
Neale, Edward Vansittart 91, 92
Neurath, Konstantin 24
Nove, Alec 73, 75

Order 1305 28, 32, 34, 41, 48, 53

Papen, Franz von 24
Pate, William 38, 44, 58
Poland 21, 22, 76

Red Army, the 17, 72, 74–9
Regulation 1A.A 60, 61
Ribbentrop, Joachim von 18, 24
Ridley, F A 133
Roosevelt, Franklin D 21, 23

Russia 7–9, 16–19, 22–5, 28, 55, 61, 72, 77, 94

Saville, John 11, 106–9
Scotland 11, 29, 59, 122
Second World War 5, 7–11, 13, 14, 23, 25, 27, 29, 30, 38, 63–5, 72–7, 97
Slovo, Joe 73
Smith, John 101
Smith, R Harris 21
Soper, Donald 97, 99
South Africa 99, 107
Spain 23, 107, 112
Stalin, Joseph 17, 18, 19, 22–77, 94, 111
Stanley, Oliver 20
Stephens, Joseph 90
Stresemann, Joachim 24
Strong, Anna Louise 73

Tawney, R H 85, 95, 97, 101
Taylor, Myrom 23
Temple, William 95–7, 100, 101
Third Reich 9, 20, 104, 105
Tomlinson, George 43
Treaty of Versailles, the 15
Trotsky, Leon 13, 21, 22, 94
Tuchachevsky, Marshal 17, 74

United States 7, 8, 10, 20, 21, 22, 23, 104, 122

Vincent, John 99
Vyshinski, Andrey 73, 74

Wehrmacht 18, 72
Weiler, Peter 106
Westcott, Bishop Brooke Foss 93
Whitehead, Major 16
Wicks, Harry 13
Wilkinson, Ellen 13, 23
Winstanley, Gerard 86, 87

Yugoslavia 76, 112